W9-BGQ-207

SIMPLE ACTS TO

Save Our Planet

500 WAYS TO MAKE A DIFFERENCE

MICHELLE NEFF

Adams Media

New York   London   Toronto   Sydney   New Delhi

▲adamsmedia

Adams Media
An Imprint of Simon & Schuster, Inc.
57 Littlefield Street
Avon, Massachusetts 02322

First Adams Media hardcover edition April 2018

ADAMS MEDIA and colophon are trademarks of Simon & Schuster.

For information about special discounts for bulk purchases, please contact Simon & Schuster Special Sales at 1-866-506-1949 or business@simonandschuster.com.

The Simon & Schuster Speakers Bureau can bring authors to your live event. For more information or to book an event contact the Simon & Schuster Speakers Bureau at 1-866-248-3049 or visit our website at www.simonspeakers.com.

Interior design by Katrina Machado
Interior images © Shutterstock/Lucky Vector; Curly Pat; Kaspri; 123RF/Macrovector; amovitania

Manufactured in the United States of America

10 9 8 7 6 5 4 3 2 1

Library of Congress Cataloging-in-Publication Data
Neff, Michelle, author.
Simple acts to save our planet / Michelle Neff.
Avon, Massachusetts: Adams Media, 2018.
Series: Simple acts.
LCCN 2017055482 (print) | LCCN 2017057723 (ebook) | ISBN 9781507207277 (hc) | ISBN 9781507207284 (ebook)
LCSH: Environmental responsibility--Handbooks, manuals, etc. | Environmental protection--Handbooks, manuals, etc. | Sustainable living--Handbooks, manuals, etc. | BISAC: NATURE / Environmental Conservation & Protection. | NATURE / Reference. | HOUSE & HOME / Sustainable Living.
LCC GE195.7 (ebook) | LCC GE195.7 .N44 2018 (print) | DDC 363.7--dc23
LC record available at https://lccn.loc.gov/2017055482

ISBN 978-1-5072-0727-7
ISBN 978-1-5072-0728-4 (ebook)

Introduction

Now is the time to take a stand and protect the earth! Every day offers opportunities to help the environment, and in *Simple Acts to Save Our Planet*, you'll find 500 easy ways for anyone and everyone to do their part in their daily lives. For instance, you could:

- Bring reusable containers to restaurants for leftovers
- Stop the junk mail by unsubscribing from all those catalogs
- Share important articles and petitions on social media
- Plant a tree (or two!) in your neighborhood
- Learn about endangered species and how to protect them
- Get your ice cream in a cone instead of a single-use cup
- Ditch the plastic bags and use a tote bag at the grocery store instead

And your influence doesn't stop there! Humans have a unique ability to alter our natural environment, and by making simple changes to the things you do every day, you can protect the planet now and make a real difference for the future. What's more, your commitment to sustainability may inspire others to take action as well! Who knows, when your coworkers see you using your own mug instead of Styrofoam cups, maybe they'll try out new travel mugs themselves. Want to make your neighborhood a bit greener? Start a compost pile to help your garden grow, and then share your strategy (and homegrown fruits and vegetables) with neighbors to spread the word.

Remember, little acts really do add up to big change. Flip through these pages and head out the door to start protecting Mother Earth!

Buy in bulk. Not only will buying items such as spices, beans, grains, dried fruits, and canned vegetables in bulk help cut down on the amount of waste produced, but you'll also save money and will eat healthier. Also, **bulk items** usually aren't loaded with preservatives to keep them fresh.

Shop at **thrift stores**. As they say, one man's trash is another man's treasure! Head down to your local thrift store to purchase gently used items that would otherwise clog up landfills. Added bonus: you can save up to 50 percent on the original price tag of designer items.

Bring a tote bag to the store. Simply by bringing a **tote bag** to the store you can help prevent hundreds of plastic bags from entering our precious oceans.

Support personal care companies that opt out of using microbeads. **Microbeads** are microscopic plastic beads typically used as exfoliating agents in beauty products. But here's the problem: they don't degrade. Because of their small size—there can be as many as 100,000 microbeads in just one squeeze of face wash—they often end up in local water treatment facilities and oceans. Help protect important marine life that might be harmed by these microbeads simply by switching products!

Unsubscribe from catalogs. Make a quick phone call to cancel catalog subscriptions, and encourage friends and family to do so too. Think of all the paper you'll save!

Use a dishwasher to **conserve water**. Rather than washing dishes by hand, an ENERGY STAR–certified dishwasher can save about 5,000 gallons of water a year!

Write to your local government representative. Pick an environmental cause you're passionate about—clean water, recycling, forest preservation—and let your representatives know how you feel. Better yet: host a **letter-writing party**.

Take **shorter showers**. Use less water by cutting back your showers by a few minutes. This is also a great way to trim your water bill!

Create a miniature greenhouse. Creating a **greenhouse** is a wonderful way to ensure that your seeds get off to a good start. If you have the space, you could even create a full-sized greenhouse and really up your gardening game!

Invest in **reusable straws**. If the trends for using plastic continue, by 2050 there will be more plastic than fish in the oceans. When a waiter asks if you would like a straw, politely decline and instead drink directly from the glass or use a stainless steel straw.

Carpool to work. This will help you save on car repair and maintenance bills in the long run, as well as provide a fun way to get to know your coworkers. **Carpooling** to work will also help save on gas, since you'll be using only one car instead of multiple cars. Win-win for you and the environment!

Shop at your neighborhood **farmers' market**. You'll be supporting your local economy and helping reduce waste, such as the fuel and packaging needed to ship food from far away!

Celebrate **Mother Earth** by planting a tree. Someday, that small sapling will grow to become an enormous tree!

🍃

Support organic beer. Conventionally grown hops are sprayed with chemical fertilizers and pesticides up to a dozen times per year. **Organic beer** is just as delicious and has a lower environmental impact. Or try brewing your own beer. Pick up a new hobby and reduce waste!

🍃

Go on a picnic to cut down on energy use at home. Get out there and enjoy the **sunshine**!

🍃

Unplug appliances when they aren't in use. No need to keep all of your appliances on when you're not even using them!

Plant **bee-friendly flowers**. Whether you live in a one-bedroom apartment with a balcony or in a large country home, you probably have room to put in at least one planter of bee-friendly flowers. Planting a pollinator-friendly garden will help attract bees and help save these vital insects! Bees love flowers that are purple, yellow, or blue, such as buttercups and clover. Bees are also attracted to flowering trees, so consider planting one if you have a larger garden.

Make sure your car headlights are efficient. Next time you're getting an oil change, ask about energy-efficient headlights, such as **LED bulbs** or laser technology.

Avoid paper towels. You can ditch paper towels altogether or opt for recycled paper towels. Using **recycled paper** also helps reduce water and energy use and saves landfill space for items that cannot be recycled.

Host a beach or river cleanup. Help keep waterways and beaches pristine and safer to enjoy by spending just a few hours cleaning up trash. Everything from cigarette butts and plastic items to food wrappers and abandoned fishing gear can all be picked up to help **keep our oceans and marine life safe**. You can host a cleanup on your own or contact your local environmental organization.

Skip red meat once a week. Meat production is placing a massive strain on the environment since it requires approximately 1,800 gallons of water to produce just 1 pound of meat. That's a whole lot of water! Knowing how resource intensive the animal agriculture industry is, you can make a huge difference by opting for a **yummy veggie burger** one night (or hey, maybe even multiple nights!) a week.

Use biodegradable dog waste bags. That's right, your pooch can be green too. When nature calls your four-legged friend, clean up the mess using a **biodegradable bag** instead of a plastic bag.

Set up your estate. You can include a bequest in your will or a living trust to an environmental group of your choosing so that a sum of your money or property can continue to **protect the environment** for many years to come!

Put up a **bat house**. Not only are they pollinators, but bats are also amazing animals to have around for insect control. One brown bat, about the size of a human thumb, can consume about 1,000 mosquitoes in just one hour. Help protect these adorable creatures by placing a bat house in your yard. You can even make your own by using old pallets, which can be found for free at some local businesses.

Host a film screening of an **environmental documentary**. Grab the popcorn and some friends and cue up *Netflix*!

Put your phone on **low power mode**. When your phone is on low power mode, the battery will last longer and you won't need to charge it as often. While some functions may take longer to complete, you'll get some extra battery life from this simple switch!

Wean yourself off palm oil. Up to 300 football fields of forests are cleared every single hour to make room for palm plantations. As a result, the orangutan population has decreased by 50 percent in just the past ten years due to habitat loss. Palm oil is commonly found in processed foods, such as cookies, ice cream, margarine, frozen pizza, crackers, pastries, candy, and chips. Palm oil can also be found in personal care and cosmetic items, so make sure to research the brands you use to see if they have committed to avoiding palm oil. If they haven't, write to the brands you love to ask them to commit to **sustainable palm oil**!

Use **all-natural cleaners**. Just as easy to use as chemical cleaners, these natural options are better for our health and the health of the planet!

🌿

Host a clothing swap. Go through your closet and put aside any items you don't use anymore. Gather some friends, grab some food, and get to swapping. When textiles decompose in landfills, they release landfill gas, which is a mix of air pollutants like carbon dioxide and methane. By hosting a **clothing swap** you'll get to hang out with your friends while preventing more clothes from entering landfills.

🌿

Keep your refrigerator out of **direct sunlight**. If you can, place your refrigerator out of direct sunlight; otherwise, the fridge will be using an excessive amount of energy to cool down. Helping the planet is as easy as considering where your refrigerator is placed in your home!

Say no to silk. Silk is made from the fibers that **silkworms** use to weave their cocoons. In order to get silk, distributers boil the worms alive while they are still inside of their cocoons. Always opt for humane alternatives, such as hemp and cotton, to help save the silkworms!

Compost. Not only is compost an awesome (and free!) fertilizer that nourishes plants and enriches soil, but it also reduces the amount of waste going to landfills. You can start a **compost pile** in a corner of your yard or opt for a compost container. Then all you have to do is collect items to compost, such as fruits, vegetables, and coffee grounds!

Opt for e-tickets. If you're traveling or going to a concert or show, choose the e-ticket version of your ticket confirmation. Typically **e-tickets** are cheaper too!

Hang up a **bird feeder**. Help our feathered friends by providing organic nuts and seeds. Just be sure not to hang the bird feeder too close to the window, so the birds don't accidentally fly into the glass!

Walk. This is the perfect way to help the environment! Instead of taking your car to run errands or go to a friend's house, walk there instead. You'll enjoy the sunshine and help reduce your carbon footprint since you're not using a car. And hey, you'll get some exercise too!

Help save grasslands. Grasslands are home to many threatened and endangered species, such as bees and butterflies. Grasslands also protect rivers from pollution and hold together healthy soils that store carbon. **Support nonprofits** that are working toward protecting our vital grasslands!

Create a butterfly garden. In addition to being beautiful, butterflies act as pollinators and as a food source for other species. **Cultivate milkweed and nectar plants** in your own garden to help protect these amazing creatures.

🍃

Be mindful of rabbit nests. Come spring, rabbits will keep their young burrowed underground. Rabbit nests are usually very well concealed among lawns, looking just like patches of dead grass to the unsuspecting eye. But underneath the grass, bunches of **baby rabbits** await their mothers. It is especially important to be aware of how inconspicuous a rabbit nest looks and to check the lawn before cutting the grass.

🍃

Invest in a **reusable tea ball**. Ditch single-use tea bags and buy bulk loose-leaf tea and a tea ball instead. Same tea, less packaging!

Plant aloe in your yard. The gel-like substance inside of an **aloe vera plant** has several uses, including treating burns, moisturizing skin, removing makeup, treating minor cuts, and sanitizing hands. Bonus: you can also drink aloe vera juice! It's commonly used to aid digestion. Instead of buying a bunch of different products, you can simply plant aloe in your yard and have one plant for many different uses. This is the perfect way to reduce consumption!

Put a **hummingbird feeder** in your yard. You'll get to witness the joy of having hummingbirds flock to your yard while protecting one of nature's most vital creatures. Make sure to fill the feeder with a mixture of between $1/4$ and $1/3$ cup of sugar (don't use honey; it ferments!) and 1 cup of water. It's also important to note that the water should not be dyed red, contrary to popular belief, because the red dye could potentially be harmful to the birds. Hummingbirds are territorial creatures, so having many small feeders with just one feeding port, rather than one large feeder with many feeding ports, is ideal.

Volunteer at a **wildlife sanctuary**. What's better than spending the afternoon helping animals in need? You'll learn about wild animals and ways you can help preserve their habitats!

Make your own soap. Many of the soaps on the market are filled with chemicals, potentially risking your health and the planet's. By making your own **yummy-smelling soap** at home you'll also eliminate wasteful packaging!

Host a yard sale. Clean out space in your closet while meeting your neighbors—and making some money too. Instead of even more clothes and household items ending up in landfills, your **yard sale** will help reusable items find new homes!

Buy **local honey**. You'll be supporting local beekeeping, which in turn supports bee populations! Buying local will also help keep the transportation costs down.

Irrigate your yard in the early morning during the summer. It's best to water your yard before the temperature begins to rise because during the heat of the day, the water is liable to easily evaporate. That means your **irrigation system** is working twice as hard to water your yard, and you're essentially throwing water away.

Use **reclaimed wood** to decorate. Got some photos from a recent vacation you want to hang up? Make an afternoon of creating your very own picture frame with scraps of wood from retired barns or old shipping crates. Not only are you reusing wood, but also your memories will be housed in a unique custom frame.

Buy a **reusable** water bottle. You'll help save marine life by keeping plastic out of the oceans.

Keep the refrigerator door closed. Can't decide what you want to eat? **Conserve energy** by keeping the fridge door closed while you decide.

Urge your government leaders to **ban ivory** in your area. Sadly, elephants are in danger of extinction; there are fewer than 650,000 elephants remaining on the planet. Poaching is one of the greatest threats these animals face, with estimates that 100 elephants are killed daily for their tusks. Help elephants simply by never purchasing ivory products, and encourage your government to take steps to protect these creatures if they haven't already!

Use a professional car wash service. Professional car wash services actually **save more water** than washing the car yourself!

Download computer software directly. If you have to update your computer, there is usually an option to purchase and **download the software directly** from the website. This way, you won't be buying a disc that you'll only use one time for the update.

Use a white roof coating to reflect the sun's light back. A white coating will **keep out excess heat**, waterproof your roof, and conserve energy. You'll be able to shave 20 to 40 percent off your annual energy bill. Not bad!

Change your voicemail message. Edit your voicemail message to include a line about the environment. For example, you could say something like, "While you're waiting for me to get back to you, please check out the issue of plastic pollution." You'll be **spreading the word** without even lifting a finger!

Use nonchemical de-icers. While ice melters are certainly convenient when we are trying to clear off our sidewalks and driveways in the wintertime, they contain harmful chemicals. What's more, salt-based products can be harmful to pets and could contaminate drinking water. Not good! Instead, look for **pet-safe, nonchemical** de-icers.

Dine by candlelight. Turn off artificial lights and use candles instead. **Energy efficient** as well as romantic!

Invest in eco-friendly sponges. To go green in your home, use a **biodegradable sponge** made out of natural and sustainable materials. Some sponges contain dyes and plastic, which are not good for our waterways and oceans. Making your home eco-friendly is not hard at all and will greatly benefit our planet!

Wash your hair less frequently. Or perhaps use dry shampoo instead of using water every day. You'll **use less water** and help prevent dangerous pharmaceuticals and personal care products (PPCPs) from entering the waterways.

Switch to low-energy security lights. Many people have security lights around their homes, but you may be able to cut back on energy use by simply switching to a **low-energy** alternative.

Recycle old car oil at a recycling depot. If you change your own car oil, make sure to **recycle the oil properly**. Oil contains lead, nickel, and cadmium, which are not healthy for our planet! Check your local requirements for safe oil disposal.

Donate seeds to a **community garden project**. Community gardens are designated areas where people plant and maintain vegetables, fruits, herbs, and flowers. Community gardens are essential for bringing fresh, healthy fruits and vegetables to food deserts and other areas that otherwise wouldn't have access to whole foods. Donate seeds (or volunteer your time!) to these crucial initiatives.

Host a Tupperware party. And when you host the Tupperware party, be sure to let guests know why they should choose reusable **Tupperware** instead of single-use bags and containers that will quickly find their way into a landfill. Further reduce your environmental footprint by hosting an online Tupperware party!

Eat what's in season. When you choose to eat with the seasons, you're automatically choosing local food, which boosts the local economy, cuts down on greenhouse gas emissions, and provides a host of benefits for your body. Eating with the season will also help you **eat mindfully**!

Paint walls a pale color so you will need less artificial light. This will help reflect the **natural light** so you'll be less dependent on artificial light. This will also help keep your home cooler in the summer months, meaning less reliance on air-conditioning!

Grow flowers to give to friends. Plant flowers in your garden so that when a special occasion rolls around, you'll have fresh, **homegrown flowers** to share instead of buying them from the grocery store. Gifting flowers you grew yourself is very thoughtful!

Switch to LED lights. One LED bulb will **lower greenhouse gas emissions** by almost half a ton compared to incandescent and compact fluorescent bulbs. You'll bring down your energy bill and help the environment at the same time.

Put your money where your heart is! Support companies with **eco-friendly policies** that help curb the destruction of our ecosystems.

Don't use blinds in your home. Heavy curtains will keep in more heat during wintertime, as well as keep the sun out during summertime. This will make your home more **energy efficient** and prevent waste since most blinds are made out of plastic.

Bring your own pillow when traveling. Most of the time when you ask for a pillow on a plane, the flight attendant will hand you one that is wrapped in plastic to help reduce the transmission of germs from one traveler to the next. Instead of asking for a pillow, **simply bring your own**. This way, you'll be reducing your plastic use even when you're thousands of miles in the sky!

Say no to dolphin hunts. There are many organizations dedicated to stopping senseless dolphin hunts; support them, and don't forget to **educate your friends and family** about dolphin hunts too. Animals are here with us on the planet, and we must protect them!

Check expiration dates. With thousands of products to choose from in shiny new packaging, it's easy to get caught up and overbuy. Try to **plan your meals** around when items will expire so you don't end up buying food that will only go in the trashcan.

Shop virtually. For some items, shopping virtually and buying in bulk may help save on time and energy that would have been spent traveling to the store.

Telecommute if you can. While not everyone has a profession where **telecommuting** is possible, if you are able to, this is a great way to cut down on harmful fuel emissions as well as your gas and car maintenance bills.

Order **small portions**. Have you ever thought about how much food waste is associated with dining out? People often order a three-course meal and then get full halfway through. When you're at a buffet, the instinct is to fill your plate high to get your money's worth. But both of these scenarios often end with perfectly good food being thrown away. Order only what you can eat!

Only run your dishwasher when it's full. It may be tempting to get dishes clean as soon as possible, but in actuality, if you run your dishwasher only when it's full, you'll help **save on energy and water**.

Brew your own coffee. Can't go without coffee? Skip your morning Starbucks trip and instead **bring your own mug** with you to the office. Think of all the cups you'll save even in just a month!

Don't go to the grocery store hungry. Easier said than done! But this is key to **preventing food waste**. Try to jot down a list of items needed at the grocery store so you don't end up picking up food that will sit in your freezer for months on end or go to waste.

Return containers for fruits and vegetables to the farmers' market. If you buy items like berries or tomatoes in little plastic containers when you go to the farmers' market, remember to **return the containers** the next time you go. This way, they will be reused and not end up as trash. Or better yet, bring your own containers!

Keep a record of your car trips to see what's necessary. It's often hard to see where our wastefulness lies. Record a diary of your trips, such as to the grocery store and running other errands, and see if you spot a pattern. Perhaps you can combine errands or cut some out altogether.

🍃

Can your own foods. Maybe you have too many tomatoes from this year's harvest and don't know what to do with them all. **Preserve this year's crop** by canning! Canning is a process in which you place fresh fruits and vegetables in jars and then heat the jars to a certain temperature to destroy microorganisms that can cause food to spoil. Canned foods also make great gifts, and you'll be cutting back on packaging waste!

Participate in **community-supported agriculture**. More commonly referred to as CSA, community-supported agriculture is a system in which community members actively support and engage in food production. Individuals and families purchase "shares" of a farm or harvest and in return receive food throughout the growing season. The "share" is usually a basket, box, or bucket of produce (or other farm goods) delivered weekly or monthly when available. Buying food this way cuts down on packaging and fuel used for delivery, and it's a big plus to know exactly where your food is coming from!

Use a stainless steel ice cube tray. If your old plastic ice trays have worn out, replace them with **stainless steel**. They work just as well and are kinder to the environment.

Use bubble wrap to insulate outdoor container plants from the cold. Got a bunch of **bubble wrap** from packages but have no idea what to do with all of it? Wrap the bubble wrap around houseplants to keep them nice and snug during wintertime.

Host a **book swap**. Get some new-to-you books while also getting rid of extra books piling up in your home! You'll be recycling old books that otherwise might have ended up in landfills.

Packaging peanuts can be used between blankets for extra warmth during cooler months. This suggestion may seem silly, but it really does work! Save those packaging peanuts and put them to good use by packing the peanuts inside your duvet cover on nights that are especially chilly.

Turn off your computer overnight. You could also put your computer in **sleep mode** to help conserve energy!

Preserve your fruit by making jam. Of course, you can pick up **local jam** from your farmers' market and help support local artisans, but making your own jam is another cheap and fun alternative.

Ask restaurants not to include utensils, napkins, and unwanted condiments when ordering takeout. If you're ordering takeout and going home or to the office to eat, chances are utensils, napkins, and condiments are already there. When placing your order, politely ask that they **forgo items you don't need**.

Cancel your gym membership and use nature as your exercise room. Between cycling, hiking, walking, and running there are tons of workouts you can do in the **fresh air**. You'll also cut back on the energy use of workout machines. Go exploring!

When buying new appliances, make sure to look for the ENERGY STAR label. This means all qualified products must meet **specific standards for energy efficiency**.

Use a water-filter pitcher or a faucet-mount filter. A million plastic bottles are bought around the world every minute. Using a filter system in your home will help reduce the need to purchase plastic bottles, which could contaminate our oceans. You could also use **activated charcoal sticks**, which naturally bond with toxins in water and can be composted after use.

Hit the trails. **Appreciate nature** by going on a hike instead of using electricity for watching TV or playing video games. Be sure to stay on the trails to prevent erosion!

Buy a laptop. Are you in the market for a new computer?
Laptops use **half as much energy** as desktop computers.
Make sure you choose a laptop with an ENERGY
STAR rating.

Empty your **dryer's lint filter** after every load. A
dirty lint filter can cause your dryer to use up to 30 percent
more energy to dry clothes. This quick fix will help
increase energy efficiency!

Turn off the faucet when brushing your teeth. This one is
really easy! When getting your pearly whites clean,
turn off the faucet so you don't waste water.

Purchase **renewable energy** from your local power company. Contact your power company and see if renewable energy (sometimes called "green" or "clean" energy) can be used to power your home. Another great way to go green!

Use an eco-friendly cutting board. Replace your old cutting board with one made of an **environmentally friendly material**, like bamboo, cork, or reclaimed wood. It's an easy way to cut back on plastic use and prevent harmful chemicals from coming into contact with your food!

Sport an eco-friendly message on your car. Adding a **bumper sticker** to your car with a message about protecting the planet is a great way to get the word out. Give people something to think about every time you drive!

Install a better showerhead. **High-efficiency showerheads** use less water than standard showerhead models.

🍃

Switch to dishwasher powder that is **biodegradable and plant-based**. Dishwasher powder can contain bleach and phosphates that harm river and marine life and can also leave a chemical residue on your dishes.

🍃

Purchase organic cotton tees. **Organic cotton** uses less water and is not treated with chemicals like pesticides. The use of chemicals in conventional cotton production has unfortunately caused environmental pollution by contaminating the water and diminishing the quality of the land.

Start a book club. Knowledge is power! Get a few friends together and start an **"environmental book club"** in your area. By reading up on the latest environmental news and issues, you'll empower yourself and others to take action for the planet!

Use biodegradable cat litter. Ever think about what happens to all that cat litter when you scoop out your four-legged friend's box? It's not a pretty sight. Using **biodegradable** cat litter will help the planet and keep your BFF happy!

Quit smoking. Not only is smoking bad for your health, but it's also bad for the planet when cigarette butts line city streets and sidewalks.

Save prescription bottles. Don't know what to do with all of those prescription bottles from the pharmacy when they are empty? You could donate them to your **local animal shelter**. Many shelters will happily reuse the prescription bottles to hold medicine for animals. Prescription bottles are also nifty for when you're traveling and need a place to store jewelry, or even to store small tacks and screws around the house. Their small size makes them quite handy, and you'll help keep them out of landfills! Helping the environment is all about creative ways to reduce and reuse!

Don't pre-rinse dishes before putting them in the dishwasher. Use decent detergent and your dishes will be just as clean while **using less water**!

Ditch the party cups. They may be convenient when hosting a get-together, but all of those **single-use cups** have to go somewhere at the end of the day, and that somewhere is the landfill. If you must use single-use cups, ask everyone to write their name on their cup so they don't need to keep getting new ones.

Use old receipts as bookmarks. Instead of buying a bunch of plastic **bookmarks**, simply use scrap pieces of paper or old receipts to hold your place in the book. Book lovers can certainly be mindful of their consumption too!

Donate your old car. Many nonprofit organizations will gladly take old cars free of charge. You'll get the old car out of the way and help contribute to the mission of a nonprofit organization working for a better world!

Try letting nature water your yard when it rains! Instead of watering your garden with the hose, this natural alternative will help you **cut back on water use**, garden efficiently, and save money.

Recycle or reuse all **newspapers**. Use newspaper as animal bedding for small mammals to prevent old papers from ending up in landfills. You can also shred the newspaper and use it to line your cat's litter box!

Use a **clothesline**. Instead of using your dryer's energy, let Mother Nature dry your clothes!

Take a shower instead of a bath. Taking a shower usually results in **less water use** than bathing. A low-flow showerhead uses about 20 gallons for a ten-minute shower, and a standard showerhead uses about 25 gallons for ten minutes. A bathtub averages about 30 gallons of water.

Use a handkerchief instead of tissues. It's bound to happen at some point: you get sick. When you do, opt for a hankie instead of paper tissues. This will keep countless tissues out of the landfill. You'll also reduce your plastic consumption since most tissue boxes have a plastic window. Simply **carry a handkerchief** around with you when you're feeling under the weather!

Turn off lights when you're not in the room. Unless you're about to come right back, there is no need to have lights on when you're not using them.

Use a **watering can** instead of a hose to water plants. That way, you'll use only the amount of water needed to water your plants.

Support bike lanes in your area. Bike lanes are designated areas on roadways for bikers to use, usually marked by signage. If your area doesn't have **bike lanes** (or if your area doesn't have enough!), support them by voicing your opinion at local city council meetings. It's important to have bike lanes if we want to encourage bikes over the use of cars for transportation.

Recycle unwanted hangers. Wire hangers are generally made out of steel and are not **recyclable**, but you can give them to your local dry cleaner so that they can reuse them.

Keep your fireplace flue damper closed when not in use. During seasons when you're not using the fireplace, keeping the damper open is essentially the same as having an open window or open door in your home, and all of the **energy** used to keep your home cool or warm will go to waste.

Say no to Styrofoam. Styrofoam takes thousands of years to break down, wreaking havoc on the planet. Instead, opt for **reusable containers** or biodegradable paper products.

Use an online directory. Opt out of a paper telephone directory in favor of an online version. If you must use a paper telephone directory, make sure you **recycle when finished**!

Go camping. **Camping** is one of the best ways to appreciate the earth and save energy you would use in your home! Forget the hustle and bustle of the city, lie out under the stars, and enjoy a relaxing campfire for a weekend. You'll feel rejuvenated, and you may learn a thing or two about the outdoors while you're at it!

Invest in a **solar oven**. Use the sun's natural energy to cook instead of having your oven exert the energy to heat up!

Sign online petitions. **Signing petitions** is quick, effective, and a great way to use your voice for good, and doing so online reduces paper waste. Don't forget to share the petitions on your social media pages to spread the message.

Reuse **plastic bags**. With the abundance of plastic bags, it's hard to stay entirely away from them. If you do end up in possession of plastic bags, give the bags a longer life by reusing them. For instance, store your bathroom plunger in a plastic bag or perhaps use one to line your garbage can. You could also check with your local recycling center to see if they accept plastic bags. There are thousands of ways we can reuse plastic bags to help protect marine life.

Soak labels off glass containers. Simply by soaking the labels off glass jars and bottles, you'll have brand-new containers to reuse around the house. A jar or bottle could hold pens and pencils on your desk, store craft items, or even display fresh-cut flowers from your garden to **brighten up your home**.

Make your own reusable heating pad. You can use old rice and a sock or a pillowcase to **make your own** heating pad by placing it in the microwave to warm. No need to buy an electric heating pad when you can make your very own at home! You'll not only be conserving energy by using a homemade reusable heating pad, but you'll also save on purchasing unnecessary products, further cutting back on packaging waste!

Reuse gift bags. Between the holidays, graduations, and birthdays, there are many occasions when gift bags, tissue paper, and other gift-wrapping items are in abundance. Save the gift bags and use them again for the next occasion.

Bring your own reusable containers to restaurants. If you're ordering food to go or have leftovers from dinner, ask the restaurant to put your meal in a **reusable container** rather than plastic you'll have to throw away later.

Rid recyclables of any food waste and use the food for your **compost pile**. Easy!

Put lights next to mirrors. The light will reflect off the mirror, and the mirror will act like a second light source. This is an innovative way to help **save on electricity** because you'll need fewer light fixtures!

Use Vaseline as lip balm. Vaseline is **helpful for healing** burns and covering abrasions, but it can also double as lip balm. Instead of buying multiple products and creating extra packaging waste, use Vaseline for a variety of purposes!

Purchase plastic-free toys for children. Kids' toys can be made out of cheap plastic that often contains harmful chemicals, such as lead. Opt for **plastic-free toys** (there are many!) instead of plastic toys that typically have short life spans and are difficult to recycle.

🌿

Choose matches over a lighter. Lighters are polluting our landfills since they are made of plastic and are filled with butane. Yuck!

🌿

Make your own dog toys. Use old rope or T-shirts to make Fido a new play toy. Keep old items out of the landfill simply by reusing them to **make something brand-new**!

Learn about the **endangered species** in your area. Learning about one or two of these animals will motivate you to help save important creatures on the brink of extinction.

Use air dryers when in public bathrooms. Most bathrooms are equipped with air dryers, so instead of using paper towels to dry your hands, shake your hands after washing and then **use an air dryer** to finish the deal.

Call before digging. If you don't, you could hit a septic tank or the protective coating of a gas line. Keep your community **free from harm** by always calling first!

Say no to glitter. Glitter, a type of microplastic, is contributing to our plastic pollution crisis. Glitter is made up of plastic and aluminum bonded with polyethylene terephthalate (PET), and the tiny specks get into everything, even water filtration systems. When these tiny plastic pieces get washed down the drain, they wind up in local watersheds. Once they get into waterways, these tiny bits act like sponges, picking up any and every environmental toxin. Only use **nonplastic, biodegradable glitters** to help protect our vital oceans and marine life!

Help prevent birds from flying into windows. Birds often fly into windows because of the reflection of trees or the sky. Thankfully, there are **many ways to help** protect them! Try putting up decals, stickers, or masking tape on the outside surfaces of your windows. You could also try mosquito screens over your windows, but ensure that the screens are on the outside of the windows and cover the entire surface. And if you happen to find one of our feathered friends after a collision, get the bird to a wildlife rehabilitator as soon as possible!

Create a Monarch Waystation. Monarch Waystations are habitats where butterflies can lay their eggs. You can buy a waystation seed kit online (or perhaps at your local gardening store) and help create waystations at your home or in parks, nature centers, schools...wherever you can think of! **Monarchs** are threatened by habitat loss, so it's crucial that we help them out!

Use old egg cartons to **grow seedlings**. Some egg cartons are not recyclable if they are made with Styrofoam, but you can easily find another use for them by planting seeds in each section. Once the seeds have sprouted, you can plant the entire egg carton in the ground if the carton is made out of biodegradable material like wood pulp or recycled paper. This is a clever way to reuse an item that would otherwise end up as trash!

Use a compostable bamboo toothbrush. Manual toothbrushes typically involve plastic materials, and electric toothbrushes don't fare much better since they're difficult to dispose of and require electricity. Bamboo is a **sustainable** material, and the toothbrush can easily break down after you get rid of it. The environment will be grateful, and your dentist will probably thank you too!

Trap and release spiders. The reaction when many of us see spiders that find their way into our homes during the colder months is to immediately kill them. However, spiders play an integral role in controlling the populations of other harmful insects. Humanely trap spiders between a glass or other container and a piece of paper and then safely place them outside. If you want to stop spiders from coming into your house try using a **peppermint or citrus essential oil spray** to deter them.

Old forks can double as **garden markers**. Watching seeds grow in your garden is very rewarding, but sometimes it's hard to tell which plant is which! You can write the names of the plants on old forks and stick them in the ground for easy marking and keep old cutlery out of the landfill at the same time.

Look for **eco-friendly paper products**. If you do purchase paper products, be sure to look for sustainable method labels, like the Green Seal Certified logo. Eco-friendly labels usually mean the paper is renewable and/or uses soy-based inks.

Avoid idling and rush hour traffic. If possible, **avoid rush hour traffic** and try to keep idling in your car to a minimum. You're burning fuel in both these situations.

Avoid rooftop carriers. If you're on a road trip, having a rooftop carrier may be essential, but when possible, try to avoid them. When carrying items on your roof, wind resistance becomes your biggest enemy and will potentially slow down your car. If you're able to avoid a rooftop carrier, you'll get **better gas mileage**.

Make sure to avoid hard stops when driving. Quick starts and hard stops **use excess gas**. If you have to stop for a stop sign or a traffic light, take your foot off the accelerator and coast before putting your foot on the brake pedal.

Don't use a single-serve coffee machine. K-Cups may be a coffee lover's dream, considering how fast and easy brewing a cup is, but the tiny plastic cups aren't **recyclable**. Think about it: if you make one cup of coffee every single day using K-Cups, that's 365 nonrecyclable cups that will enter our landfills. Luckily, an eco-friendly alternative is just as simple: when using a French press, all you have to do is scoop the ground coffee, add some water, and press down on the lid to pour.

Open car windows when driving at slow speeds, and use air-conditioning when on highways. This will help you get **better gas mileage**!

Support fair trade. Many consumers have long been advocates of fair trade, the socially conscious decision to support sustainable clothing, food, and other items. By looking for the Fair Trade Certified logo on items, you'll be supporting fair pay and working conditions for farmers and producers, as well as eco-friendly practices that work to minimize our environmental footprint.

Collect melted wax to **make your own candles**. Instead of purchasing new candles, compile all of the wax from melted candles and make a brand-new candle yourself. This will save the planet from even more waste, and you'll save money too!

Ask your hotel to not change towels and sheets every day. Traveling? Most hotels now have environmentally friendly policies in place where staff don't change towels and sheets every day in an effort to **cut back on water use**. If they don't, politely ask the front desk to skip your room or hang a "do not disturb" card on your doorknob so cleaning staff members know to skip your room!

Host a zero-waste party. Inspire your friends and family by hosting a **zero-waste party**. Use a cloth tablecloth, plan a waste-free menu, and decorate with materials you already have in the house!

Invest in an eco-vacuum. There are many **eco-vacuums**, including options that are bagless or ones with high-efficiency particulate air (HEPA) filters, that will reduce not only electricity use but also electricity cost!

Go dairy-free. On average, a cow can drink 23 gallons of water a day. As a result, the dairy industry uses a huge amount of water just to hydrate the cow, in addition to the water used to keep the facilities and milking equipment clean. If you chose to replace your two scoops of dairy ice cream for a **dairy-free** alternative, you could save 84 gallons of water!

Avoid steel-jaw traps. Steel-jaw traps are widely used to trap **wild animals** for their fur and are anything but humane. They are banned or restricted in many US states, and the European Union has banned their use in Europe. Painfully trapping innocent animals is anything but kind to the earth's other inhabitants. Don't support the use of steel-jaw traps!

Say no to fur. Aside from the animal welfare implications, the production of fur garments requires about twenty times **more energy** than that of fake fur garments. In addition, the chemicals used on them prevent them from biodegrading, so when these furs are no longer considered in style, they end up buried in landfills.

Invest in a non-disposable razor. Using disposable razors just means more non-biodegradable plastic ending up in our landfills and oceans. It may seem like a bit more money at first, but investing in a **non-disposable** razor will be beneficial to all in the long run.

Say no to plastic mailboxes. It seems like everywhere you turn nowadays plastic is there. Even mailboxes are made out of plastic! When you're in need of a new mailbox, consider purchasing a green mailbox, such as one made out of aluminum. This is a simple way to **reduce your plastic use**!

Skip plastic stirrers. Ever order a cocktail and the bartender gives you the drink with a plastic stirrer? For the most part, cocktail stirrers only add to the aesthetic appeal of the drink and aren't needed. When you order your drink, politely ask the bartender to leave out the stirrer. Help **prevent unnecessary plastic waste**!

Invest in clean energy through the stock market. Global energy demand continues to rise, and by investing in renewable energy, you'll prove to be an advocate for the environment. Talk to an investor for advice on getting started!

Use Edison bulbs. They look just like vintage Edison incandescents but instead use LEDs. Get that old-timey feel, but **use less energy** doing so!

Go vegan or vegetarian. Raising animals for food is taking an enormous toll on our planet's resources. The global livestock system accounts for a staggering 23 percent of global freshwater consumption and 45 percent of total land use. If that wasn't enough, the animal agriculture industry is one of the largest drivers of deforestation and is responsible for more greenhouse gas emissions than the entire transportation sector. Simply swapping foods you love with **plant-based alternatives** is a great way to cut your carbon footprint in half!

Opt for plastic-free shoes. Choose shoes made out of **natural materials**, such as hemp, or buy shoes secondhand so you won't be contributing to unnecessary plastic waste.

Bring reusable produce bags to the grocery store. Ever notice how many plastic bags you take from the produce section of the grocery store? You can easily make your own **reusable produce bags** using old T-shirts, organic cloth, or even mesh to take with you to the store.

Write to companies. If a company is doing something not so nice to the environment, write to them and **let them know**! Most companies have a contact form option on their website, but posting on their *Facebook* pages and tweeting at them about why you are concerned are also good ways to get their attention.

Use paper that has wildflower seeds embedded in it. Yep, paper you can plant is a thing! When you plant the paper in a pot of soil, a wildflower will grow. You can use this innovative paper for wedding invitations, printer paper, or promotional products. Just remind recipients to plant it instead of throwing it out! With bee populations in severe decline, **planting wildflowers** will help increase their habitat and food supply.

Travel in a group. Plan a trip with friends and you're likely to reduce your carbon footprint by **carpooling**, using public transportation, and/or buying in bulk.

Use *AmazonSmile* to **donate** to your favorite environmental groups. If you shop through *AmazonSmile*, which has the same products and prices as *Amazon*, then 0.5 percent of your purchase will be donated to a charitable group of your choosing.

Recycle your pet's collar and leash. Donate old pet accessories to your local animal shelter instead of having them end up in landfills. When purchasing new collars and leashes, look for ones made out of hemp. Hemp is a **sustainable crop** with the ability to grow in a variety of climates and soil types. Choosing hemp when possible is the green way to go!

Only photograph animals from a respectful distance. With the popularity of social media sites on the rise, taking photos with animals has become a widespread trend. Unfortunately, there have been many cases where human interference, all to get a selfie, has negatively affected animals. Remember to always leave **wildlife** out of the picture!

Share informative articles on your social media. See an article about plastic pollution? Is an animal on the verge of extinction? **Share it** on your social media pages! The more people know about environmental issues, the better.

Install **solar walkway lights** instead of floodlights. Solar walkway lights charge throughout the day and then run off the stored energy at night. You'll be able to light up your walkway with no additional energy consumption!

Support **eco-tourism**. Traveling is a wonderful way to learn about a new culture and see different sights, but responsible travel should always be a priority. You can travel to areas that help conserve the environment and improve the well-being of community members.

Ask for **no receipts** at the store. Nine times out of ten, guess where that receipt is going to end up? In the trashcan. If you're not expecting to return an item, ask for no receipt when the cashier is checking out your items, or ask for the receipt to be emailed if you think you'll need a copy.

Use nonplastic reusable utensils. Every environmentalist should have a reusable bamboo utensil set! **Bamboo** is highly durable, and considering how fast growing and renewable it is, it's a sustainable product to produce. Plus, think of all the plastic utensils you could prevent from entering our landfills!

Try to avoid fast food. It may be quick and cheap, but fast food creates tons of excess trash—and there are plenty of healthier, more **environmentally friendly options** that are just as tasty! Try to bring food from home if you know you're going to be on the go.

Invest in **sensor lights** in your home. This way, lights will turn on only when you are in the room, which will help conserve energy!

Don't use weed killers. Guess where all of those chemicals go? Into our **waterways**!

Make your own **Halloween costume**. Either make your own or research costume shops in your area where you can rent a costume for Halloween. Looking for used costumes is another option to help cut back on unnecessary purchases and package waste!

Use biodiesel. Biodiesel is a **renewable fuel source** developed from vegetable and animal fats. Depending on the type of car you drive, biodiesel could help create fewer greenhouse gas emissions than petroleum-based fuels. You can find biodiesel at your local retail gas station.

Share a taxi or Uber with someone. Perhaps your coworker also needs a ride, or maybe you're next to a stranger who is looking for a taxi too. Whatever the case may be, **share a ride** with someone to save on gas.

Buy used furniture. If you're in the market for a new sofa, consider going to your local thrift store or Habitat for Humanity store to see what furniture they have in stock. Furniture-making involves many harmful chemicals, and by buying used you'll be helping your health as well as the **health of the planet**!

Use a rain barrel in your yard. Rain barrels have increased in popularity over the years as clean water sources have become scarcer. In fact, some parts of the world are set to run out of fresh water in the next century, perhaps even the next decade, and over 2.1 billion people already lack access to clean drinking water. By placing a rain barrel in your yard to catch **rainwater**, you can use the water to wash your car, water your garden, or even do household chores like wash the dishes. When free water falls from the sky, you might as well use it!

Join a local tool library. Many cities have what is known as a tool library, where you pay a yearly fee and are able to "borrow" tools, just as you would a book from the library. This is a great way to support your local community's economy while reducing the number of tools you need to buy. Or simply start your own tool share by introducing yourself to your neighbor and offering to trade power equipment for your lawn care needs. You'll be supporting a **sustainable community** right in your neighborhood, and you won't have to buy a dozen power tools with heavy packaging when it's possible to simply rent or borrow one when needed.

Teach kids how to be eco-friendly. It's our job to teach the next generation how to be kinder to the planet. Simple lessons on the dangers of plastic pollution, the importance of marine life, and the value of planting trees will help lay the foundation for **future environmental leaders**.

Use bamboo for flooring and construction. In some cases, bamboo can grow 3 to 4 feet per day without the need for fertilizers, pesticides, or much water. Bamboo is so **fast growing** that it can yield twenty times more timber than trees in the same exact area.

Use your local public library. Take advantage of all the books, magazines, and electronic resources your library has to offer! For hundreds of years, the library has been the cornerstone of a sustainable community, offering a place for people to expand their knowledge of the world around them. Many neighborhoods also have **"little free libraries"** in yards and on street corners where you can borrow books and recycle your old books. If your area doesn't have a free library, make one!

Clean a storm drain. Be aware of a storm drain near your house and keep trash out of the surrounding area. Think of all the trash you could save from ending up in our **waterways and oceans**!

Use the first in, first out method. A handy trick to help reduce food waste is to move older products to the front of your refrigerator so you eat them first. **Saving our planet** is as easy as being organized!

Start a new holiday tradition by hosting a **potluck**. Cut back on excess cooking and cleaning, and try a new family dish from a friend!

Create art with pressed leaves and flowers. Have you ever been taking a walk and seen a beautiful leaf or flower on the ground? One way to **preserve the beauty of nature** is by creating pressed art to hang in your home. There are many free tutorials online on how to create your own unique pressed art!

Support **national parks**. With hundreds of government-protected national parks all around the world, there is no shortage of beautiful parkland to explore. Plus, your entrance fee helps maintain the park. Create a bucket list and start planning your visit!

Get electronics **repaired** when possible. Don't throw the electronics out so they add to waste in landfills—fix the problem instead!

Change your email signature. You could include a favorite quote about the environment, a website for people to check out, or perhaps a fact about animal extinction. Whatever you choose, every time someone emails you, they'll be reminded of **important environmental issues**!

Support organizations that are helping rebuild coral reefs. Although **coral reefs** are the lifelines of our oceans, they are unfortunately dying and creating an ecological domino effect on marine life. Not only are coral reefs home to approximately 4,000 species of fish, but they also act as buffers against wave action and prevent erosion along the shoreline. Spread the word and support groups advocating for coral reefs!

Keep gum off sidewalks and roads. If you enjoy gum, keep a tissue or **scrap piece of paper** in your pocket or in the car so you don't end up tossing the gum on the sidewalk or road.

Buy movies online instead of buying DVDs. Most, if not all, movies can be purchased online nowadays. Help cut back on the use of plastic to make DVD cases and reduce the clutter of DVDs in your home at the same time!

Use sea salt, not ground table salt. Usually table salt is mined from underground salt deposits, while **sea salt** is produced by evaporating ocean water or water from saltwater lakes. With sea salt there is usually very little processing involved. Or better yet, avoid salt entirely and season your food with herbs!

Use a reusable sandwich container for kids' lunches. Minimize waste by **avoiding plastic sandwich bags**. You'll also be teaching kids about responsibility, since they will have to bring the container home from school every day!

Join a **watchdog group** for your community. Such groups will watch what power companies do, for instance, and come up with strategies for fighting policies that are unfriendly to the environment.

Leave wildlife alone. Human intervention can sometimes do more harm than good. Always call your local wildlife rehabilitation center if you see a wild animal that is injured. You may even want to put the number for your **local wildlife rehabilitator** in your phone for easy access in times of emergency.

Don't keep wildlife as pets. Baby animals may be adorable, but purchasing **exotic animals**, such as tigers, lemurs, and lions, to keep as pets fuels the illegal wildlife trade.

Use a **metal pet dish** instead of plastic. Metal is easier to clean and is very eco-friendly!

Carry nutritious bird food. When ducks, geese, swans, and other waterfowl ingest a diet too high in protein or carbohydrates, they can develop a very serious condition that has been dubbed "angel wing." The disorder causes the last joint in one or both wings to unnaturally twist outward, rather than lying flat against the bird's body. You can still bond with waterfowl, but instead feed them the right food to sustain their health. Nutritious waterfowl feed and duck pellets are both inexpensive and easy to carry. You could also feed waterfowl seedless grapes cut in half; shredded kale, Swiss chard, or romaine lettuce; and grains, including wheat, barley, and oats. Properly feeding birds will also help children understand how to **compassionately coexist with wildlife**.

Go on a local eco-tour. Your local wildlife center may offer tours about native plants and wildlife. Learn about our **amazing planet** from the experts!

Use natural gas instead of charcoal for grilling. Charcoal produces tiny particles that pollute the air. By using propane or natural gas instead of charcoal, you won't be contributing to air pollution. Better yet, use an **electric grill** that is powered by the sun or wind and you'll really be grilling green!

Say no to plastic loofahs. Instead of purchasing a plastic loofah, opt for an **eco-friendly sponge** made out of bamboo or other natural fibers. Whenever possible, we should choose sustainable products to help our planet!

Keep lights off during turtle nesting season. If you live near a turtle nesting area, try to keep artificial lights off. This way you'll reduce light pollution that affects **sea turtles** during nesting season when they are trying to find a quiet, dark place to release their eggs. Artificial lighting near shorelines distracts mother turtles and can cause hatchlings to become confused and wander inland. Some coastal communities worldwide have even passed ordinances that require residents to turn off beachfront lights during the season.

Get metal-framed glasses instead of plastic frames. You can even **say no to plastic** with your eyewear!

Protect the elephants. Between poaching, the tourism industry, and habitat loss, both **African and Asian elephants** are in danger of becoming extinct. Avoid tourist attractions that offer interactions with elephants, and help educate others about the dangers elephants face when kept in captivity.

Rotate garden crops. If you keep planting the same crops in your garden every season, it will create an imbalance in the soil nutrients. Make sure to change up crop choices and locations to help with soil fertility and improve your crop yield.

Go on a **whale-watching** tour. You'll want to ensure that the tour is eco-friendly and the whales aren't harmed, but a whale-watching tour is a great way to see these magnificent creatures in their natural habitat!

Don't throw confetti at parties. Parties can certainly be a lot of fun, but throwing **confetti** only creates unnecessary trash.

Recycle cell phones. Find an "ecoATM," where you can recycle cell phones for cash. Considering that electronics contain materials that can pose risks to human health and the environment, it's important to divert cell phones from entering landfills!

Stay off sand dunes. You've probably seen signs at the beach that say, "Stay off the dunes," and they are there for good reason. **Sand dunes** can erode very quickly and are held in place by fragile plants. If you destroy the dunes by running or walking on them, you could cause the plants to die and further increase the erosion, throwing the natural ecosystem off balance.

Avoid powerboats. If possible, try to steer clear of powerboats because they could negatively affect aquatic **ecosystems** by disturbing fish and wildlife, destroying plants, and contributing to soil erosion.

Use paper clips, not staples. Staples offer one-time use, whereas you can reuse a **paperclip** over and over again.

Find an **eco-friendly dry cleaner**. Many dry cleaners are now committed to reducing water waste and decreasing the use of perchloroethylene (or "perc"), a hazardous air pollutant. Ask your dry cleaner if they are environmentally friendly, and if not, suggest ways they could be.

Use string to keep your hair up instead of buying elastic or rubber bands. String will do the job just as well, and you'll be further **reducing your consumption** by not buying hair bands!

Install a low-flow toilet. It will use significantly **less water** than a full-flush toilet, which will both benefit the planet and save you money on your water bill.

Use reusable menstrual products. It's true; you can even help our planet when it's that time of the month! Disposable products end up in landfills, so opt for **reusable products** like cloth pads and menstrual cups instead.

Use **natural mosquito repellents**. Mosquitoes may be annoying, but there are plenty of simple, natural preventative measures available. A citronella plant can work in place of a mosquito-repellent candle. Peppermint oil and the oil from a catnip plant can also be used to avoid mosquitoes.

Enjoy life under the sea by going **scuba diving**. Just remember not to take anything; only look to appreciate the beauty!

Stop using **balloons**. They may be beautiful to watch float up into the air, but balloons harm wildlife. When they finally descend, 70 percent of the time they end up in the ocean. Animals both on land and in the oceans frequently mistake deflated balloons for food.

Use **aluminum cans** instead of steel. Aluminum is one of the easiest metals for consumers to recycle. Generally, cans (such as soup cans and canned fruits and vegetables) are marked as aluminum, and steel is usually heavier.

Opt for a cloth interior in your car. If you're in the market for a new or used car, consider one with a **cloth interior** rather than leather. There are many toxic chemicals that are used in the process of creating leather that can spill into our waterways.

Check out **waterfalls** in your area. Pick a waterfall you've never been to and make an afternoon out of appreciating its beauty.

Don't burn plastic. Burning plastic may seem like a better alternative to leaving plastic in landfills, but in truth, burning releases toxic chemicals into the air. The best option is to try to not use plastic at all!

Be careful with wood when making campfires. You'll want to be careful with the fire itself, of course, but be mindful of who may be living near or around the **wood** you're picking up!

Forage for food. Take advantage of what nature has to offer and encourage healthy eating by foraging for foods like berries, herbs, lettuce, and mushrooms. Contact a local **foraging expert** to show you where to find the best foods and how to avoid the dangerous ones!

Don't buy travel-sized items. You can just as easily use **small glass containers** to hold shampoo and other toiletries when you're traveling.

Invest in a **digital thermometer** to avoid mercury. If the mercury spills or the vapors are inhaled after a thermometer is broken, it can be toxic to both you and the planet. Don't risk it!

If you live around bears, be careful with trash. During the summer months, bears are hungry and will roam to find food. Purchase a **bear-resistant trash container** to ensure the safety of both people and bears.

Take a **nature photography** class. Learn a new skill while celebrating the outdoors! Take a class on how to capture nature's beauty and you'll more than likely have a greater appreciation for all of Mother Nature.

Use essential oils to make your own perfume. Using a mixture of just a few essential oils along with a carrier oil, you can create your very own unique **perfume**!

Rid your home of ants **naturally**. Don't immediately go for the death traps! Follow the ants back to the root source and use mint, cinnamon, coffee grounds, red chili powder, cloves, or rosemary to dissuade them.

Avoid single-use items. Plastic bags, cups, and utensils probably come to mind first when you think of how you can **reduce your plastic waste**, but there are other single-use items that we need to remember. Most of the time, cotton swabs and balls are only used for a few seconds and then are tossed in the trash. See what single-use items you can eliminate in your daily life!

Reuse old socks or T-shirts for cleaning. Instead of throwing them out, **reuse old clothes** for car cleaning or even for general cleaning around the house.

Avoid fireworks. Fireworks can certainly be pretty, but the loud noises scare both wild and domestic animals. The noise creates fear, stress, and anxiety in animals, causing them to flee the noise and end up in other unsafe areas like highways. The other downside of fireworks: **the environmental impact**. Fireworks can cause fires and release poisonous chemicals that are inhaled by wildlife and that contaminate the environment. Because of the numerous adverse effects of fireworks, many cities worldwide have opted for laser light shows instead.

Keep your fridge free from frost. A buildup of frost and ice only drives up your **energy use**. Check your freezer occasionally to see if there is unnecessary frost.

Don't put hot food in the fridge. Putting hot food in the fridge makes the fridge work overtime trying to cool it down. Let it cool to **room temperature** before putting the food in the fridge.

Use a shaker ball for mixed drinks or smoothies. Put away your electric mixer to **conserve more energy**!

Say no to dryer sheets. They may be convenient, but dryer sheets and fabric softeners contain chemicals that could harm your health, damage the environment, and pollute the air. Instead use a **reusable dryer ball** and some essential oils when drying your clothes, and voilà! You'll have fresh-smelling clothes, free of static and wrinkles.

Get your kids outside! There are plenty of activities to enjoy outside, like biking, taking a hike, and learning about wildlife. Not only will the kids learn to **appreciate nature**, but more time outside means less time using electricity playing video games and watching TV. Win-win!

Plant shrubs and/or trees instead of building a fence. If you're thinking of building a fence around your property, consider planting shrubs and/or trees instead. They will act as a **natural barrier**—and be really pretty!

Make your own bread. **Making bread at home** lets you control what you put into your bread and therefore your body. Plus, think of all the plastic packaging you'll keep out of landfills!

Do yoga. Yoga is relaxing, can provide core exercise, and has a low environmental impact since you don't need any bulky machinery. You could even go to your favorite hiking spot and **do yoga outside**. You'll be reducing the consumption of needless exercise equipment in favor of using what nature already provides!

Learn about snakes. Snakes may be misunderstood members of the animal kingdom, but they are actually a vital part of our ecosystem. Small snakes, for example, will feed on harmful bugs and insects. Larger snakes will eat mice, rats, and other small mammals that could potentially destroy crops. And if snakes weren't around, the predators that eat snakes wouldn't be able to find food, throwing the ecosystem out of balance. Spend the day at your **local wildlife center** learning about these amazing animals!

Carbonate your own drinks. There are many **do-it-yourself** ways to carbonate your own beverages, but you can also buy a soda or seltzer maker if you're new to the process. If you enjoy soda, carbonating your own drinks will help cut back on aluminum can and plastic bottle waste—and you'll learn a new skill!

Don't buy down products. Down is the soft layer of feathers closest to the bird's skin; it's often used in pillows, bedding, and jackets. Thankfully, there are many **cruelty-free** options that don't involve hurting our feathered friends. When shopping for a new pillow or bedding, look for a cotton down alternative.

Learn how your town recycling system works. Being an effective advocate for the planet means understanding what can and cannot be recycled and how the process works. Contact your **local recycling system** to learn about your city's program!

Be careful about what you flush. It may be easy to toss stuff in the toilet or down the sink without thinking twice, but needlessly flushing items down the toilet could back up your sewer system, as well as cause **environmental pollution** and corrupt your community's water. For instance, old medications, baby wipes, kitty litter, and coffee grounds should never be flushed down the toilet!

Petition your city to install LED streetlights. LED streetlights require only half of the power consumption and typically produce the **same amount of light**. If your city doesn't already have LED streetlights, send a polite message to your local city council asking for a switch.

❧

Buy cloth lawn chairs instead of plastic. **Cloth lawn chairs** will last longer, and you won't be contributing to plastic pollution. Win!

❧

Use **water purification** tablets when camping. These tablets kill microorganisms in water to prevent water-borne diseases. Being able to purify water while camping, hiking, or traveling will allow you to use local waterways instead of having to rely on bottled water.

Join your local YMCA or YWCA. Most offer area **cleanup** projects, such as picking up trash at a nearby park, but most also offer outdoor activities for kids. And you may just make a new friend along the way!

Ferment foods. Not only will fermenting your food to make sauerkraut, kimchi, kombucha, miso, and other items help preserve the food, but fermented foods have long been touted for their **health benefits**. Fermenting vegetables will increase their nutritional value, benefit your digestive tract, and promote good oral and dental health. And no food goes to waste!

Properly dispose of Christmas trees. After the holiday celebrations, instead of placing your Christmas tree on the curb for the garbage truck to pick up, you can use the tree for **mulch or compost**. There's no need to further crowd landfills when your Christmas tree can serve other purposes!

Experiment with new recipes. Get creative in the kitchen! Using the microwave less and avoiding heavily packaged products doesn't have to be a dull endeavor. You might even save on gas since you're not going out to eat at a restaurant. Find a **new recipe** you've never tried before and have fun cooking!

Participate in public speaking. If there is a group in your area that helps members improve their **public speaking skills**, sign up! When asked to do a speech, present information on an environmental issue you're passionate about. By participating in the group, you'll learn how to effectively communicate, and you'll also help educate others in the group who might not have known about that particular issue. When saving the planet, sometimes you have to get creative in order to spread the word about important issues!

Opt for an ice cream cone over a cup. You may not think you can be green while at the ice cream shop, but you can! Order your **ice cream in a cone** so you'll create zero container and utensil waste. You'll save tons of single-use cups from polluting our planet!

Use leaves as compost. Not only are all of those leaves that drop during the autumn season beautiful, but you can also use them as compost! Shred the leaves using a shredder or a lawn mower and add the leaves to your compost bin or pile. It is also worthwhile to add **fresh-cut grass clippings** to the leaves, as the nitrogen will help break down the leaves faster. Instead of putting bags of leaves out to be picked up on trash day, reuse what nature already provides to reduce your impact on the planet!

Use cardboard boxes to kill weeds. Place a cardboard box over the area and hold it down with a heavy object, like a rock. The box will prevent any light from reaching the weeds. Cardboard is **biodegradable** and you're not using any weed killers, which contain heavy chemicals that are unfriendly to our waterways.

Use a **digital photo frame**. You'll still be able to preserve your memories, but instead of buying a dozen photo frames, you can simply use one digital frame.

Create a library display. Public libraries will usually have a display case to feature posters and leaflets on important issues. Visit your **local library** and add materials to educate others about environmental issues important to you, such as plastic pollution or global warming. You could also ask your local natural-food store if they would make space in their window display. Spread the word and encourage people to take action!

Put a **bee house** in your yard. Bees are responsible for pollinating hundreds of different agricultural plants, making them crucial to a sustainable food system. You can buy a bee house from your local gardening store or try making one yourself. This will help provide bees with a nesting area, as well as give you a neat way to learn about these amazing animals!

Properly put out campfires. Always ensure that fires are put out completely to prevent **wildfires** that could threaten the wildlife.

If you live on a lake, stream, or wetland, plant a buffer strip of native plants along the water. Buffers provide food and **habitat for wildlife** while also removing pollutants by naturally absorbing them. By simply creating a buffer strip, you can help your local ecosystem!

Choose **cloth diapers**. If you have a little one, invest in cloth diapers instead of disposable ones. Disposable diapers can take 500 years to decompose in the landfill, while cloth diapers can be washed and reused and contain fewer chemicals.

Don't litter. This one should be a no-brainer, but people continue to litter on sidewalks and on the sides of roads. Mother Nature isn't a trashcan; **let's keep her clean**!

🍃

Screenprint your own shirts. Instead of buying new shirts, take old T-shirts or ones bought from thrift stores and **screenprint** unique designs onto them. You can easily screenprint at home and help reduce the number of clothing items in the landfill.

🍃

Wash your car on the grass. Plants, mulch, and soil will **naturally remove pollutants** from water runoff, but if you wash your car on the driveway, the water will go directly into the storm rain, eventually leading to waterways like lakes and rivers.

Sweep or rake away from street curbs. Otherwise, all of the grass and leaves will clog the curbs and storm drains and go into lakes and rivers. The nutrients will promote unwanted algae growth, and when the algae decompose at the bottom of the lake, they will use up the oxygen that fish and native plants need to survive. **Be mindful** of where you are sweeping grass and leaves and Mother Nature will appreciate it!

Never dump waste into a storm drain. Storm sewers run directly to rivers and lakes. Only **rainwater** should go down storm drains to keep the earth healthy!

Sponsor an animal at a local wildlife rehabilitation center. The goal of these centers is to rehabilitate sick or injured wildlife so that eventually they can be returned to the wild. Pick your favorite wildlife rehabilitation center and sponsor one of the animals in their care. Your sponsorship will help provide food, medication, veterinary care, supplies, and bedding for one of the animals.

Get moving boxes from the grocery store. Instead of buying a ton of **moving boxes** from your local home-improvement store, many grocery stores will give you boxes free of charge. All you have to do is ask! This is a great way to cut back on excessive cardboard use.

Try bird watching. Learn more about the animals that share our planet! Grab your binoculars and a current field guide and head out to watch our **feathered friends** for the afternoon.

Buy bulk shampoo. Bring your own glass containers to your local health-food store to buy your shampoo in bulk. There are other toiletries, such as conditioner and liquid soap, that you can **buy in bulk** too. Think of all the plastic bottles you'll be keeping out of landfills!

Never purchase products made from threatened or endangered species. If you are traveling and see tortoiseshell, coral, or any other product made from a threatened or endangered species, don't buy it! By doing so, you'll be supporting the illegal wildlife trade and hurting **threatened or endangered animals**.

Attract **ladybugs** to your garden. Ladybugs are very beneficial to a garden because they help get rid of destructive pests, like mites and aphids. To attract ladybugs to your garden, try planting cilantro, chives, dill, or fennel. Don't forget to eliminate the use of insecticides, which are harmful to the ladybugs!

Reuse envelopes. It's hard to avoid envelopes altogether, but you can save them and reuse old ones for taking notes. You can do the same with junk mail or unwanted event fliers. It's important to always reuse when possible!

Upgrade home insulation. You can save money by upgrading your home with **energy-efficient** insulation. Wall insulation can cut heat loss through the wall by up to 60 percent. Better yet, you'll reduce the amount of energy used in your home!

Take a horticulture class at your local college. Learn more about **plant conservation** and other gardening tips. You'll likely meet other environmentalists in the class as well as learn how to be the best gardener you can be!

Go **stargazing**. Take a blanket and some binoculars and head out at night to stargaze. You'll come away with a greater appreciation for our planet and a greater understanding of why it's so important to speak up for the earth!

Install new storm windows. Storm windows can keep the temperature consistent inside your house by reducing air movement, thereby lowering cooling and heating costs. That means **less energy** spent heating and cooling your home!

Set a sleep timer on your TV. Sometimes we leave the TV on all night, not even realizing until the next morning that we've done so. Set a **sleep timer** and save on electricity use!

Switch to a **refillable pen**. Instead of buying a packet of pens every few months, invest in a refillable pen and buy the ink separately whenever you need more. If you work in an office, ask your boss if the office can switch to refillable pens too. All of the pens really do add up in our landfills!

Use coffee grounds and tea bags in your garden. After you have a cup of tea or coffee, use the **tea bag or coffee grounds** in your garden and compost bin. They'll act as added fertilizer in place of boxed fertilizers from your local garden store. Tea bags will also serve as an organic way to repel pests!

Replace battery-operated flashlights with hand-crank LED alternatives. No need to recharge or buy new **batteries**!

Visit your local nature center. **Nature centers** are usually kid-friendly and offer a hands-on approach to learning about the natural world. What better way to save our planet than by studying the awe-inspiring nature all around us? Plus, staff members may be able to give you tips for more things you can do right at home to help the planet!

Upcycle boxes. You can use old shoeboxes as storage containers for photos or crafts, and empty cereal boxes can easily be made into magazine holders. Try using old boxes to ship things, or **add a little imagination** for some fun with the kids (big boxes can be used to make forts!). When we get creative and reuse items, it puts less strain on the planet!

Take a **furniture-repair** class. When a piece of furniture breaks or is torn, you'll be able to salvage it instead of immediately taking it to the dump. Learning how to repair upholstery and wood could add years to the life of your furniture, and you can help extend the life of your friends' and family's furniture too!

Use old T-shirts to make a **memory blanket**. Another great way to reuse! Take old event T-shirts and sew them together to make a warm blanket that will remind you of your favorite activities. Suggest that your friends and family members do the same. It could prevent tons of T-shirts from ending up in landfills!

Clean up after your dog. Not only is it polite to pick up after your dog, but dog waste also contains bacteria that aren't so nice for the environment. And where exactly does all of that waste go if you don't pick it up? Right into the drain and then off to our waterways. Be a good dog guardian and an **advocate for the planet** by picking up after your dog!

Don't feed wildlife. While some waterfowl are domestic or semi-domestic and can be fed safely, many other wild animals cannot. If you see a fox on a hike, for instance, don't try to feed it. It's important for **wildlife** to not become dependent on humans!

Use poo paper. It's exactly what it sounds like: paper made from the waste of animals, such as elephants and sheep. It's **recycled and fair trade**! If you need paper for invitations, your work office, or kids' crafts, consider looking into poo paper.

Make your own **vegetable broth**. Save your cooking leftovers and make a broth out of the vegetable scraps by sautéing the scraps and then simmering them with water, herbs, and spices!

Use your **ceiling fan**. You can use a ceiling fan to circulate air in the summer months, meaning your air-conditioning won't have to work as hard. It's a pretty easy way to help the earth while saving on electricity costs!

Plant seeds from last season. **Save seeds** from your garden and plant them during the next rotation. No need to waste perfectly good seeds; plus, you'll save on buying new seeds every season.

Plant only native plants. Since every ecosystem is different, planting **native plants** in your yard and garden is the best way to help wildlife. Planting exotic plants could lead to invasive species, which could take over the area.

Properly dispose of printer ink and toner cartridges. Once the cartridges are empty, call your local office supply store or recycling center to find the best way to recycle them. This will help our planet because the plastic used in cartridges won't **biodegrade** in landfills. Another option is to buy a printer cartridge refill kit and reuse old cartridges.

Help protect ants. When ants dig tunnels, they aerate the soil and recycle nutrients, which is really important for the health of the soil and **plant growth**. Ants also help reduce the need for chemical fertilizers and irrigation. Ants even aid in decomposition and turn up more soil than earthworms. Amazing, right? Next time you see some ants, be thankful for their service to our environment!

Add more beans to your diet. Save money and fight climate change simply by **eating beans**. If we all ate beans instead of beef as our primary source of protein, we could free up 42 percent of the cropland we currently use to grow feed for cows. Growing crops for humans instead would help give habitat back to wildlife.

Use a smart power strip. Setting up your entertainment center with a power strip makes it easier when it's the end of the night and you want to turn everything off at once. You could also upgrade to a smart power strip, which will sense when a device is not in use and will automatically shut power off. An easy way to **reduce energy use**!

Keep your car covered in the winter. Not only will having your car covered make it easier to clear off when it snows, but your car also won't be as cold on the inside. This means **less time and energy** spent warming it up!

🌿

Use a cloth shower liner. Instead of buying plastic shower liners, buy a cloth one and simply throw it in the wash when it gets dirty. This is a simple way to help **reduce plastic pollution**!

🌿

Visit a science museum. Spend an afternoon at your local **science museum** learning about our planet. You'll not only learn something new, but you'll also come away with a greater understanding of the earth and how things work!

Keep track of your trash for a week. By keeping track of your trash for one week, you'll uncover some surprises about your habits. For instance, in one week you can look at single-use items, such as plastic utensils and cotton balls, and see how much trash you're really contributing to the planet. See what you can do without and make changes accordingly.

Use pizza boxes for car maintenance. If you ordered pizza delivery, don't waste the box! **Pizza boxes**, as well as other cardboard boxes, can be broken down to lay flat underneath a car when you're changing the car's oil. Pizza for dinner, a clean garage floor, and you're helping the environment by preventing waste!

Use a cloth tablecloth instead of plastic. If you're getting ready for a party, consider buying a **cloth tablecloth** so you won't be purchasing yet another plastic item that will just end up in the trash.

Recycle **contact lenses**. Yep, you can recycle contact lenses! Contact your local recycling center to see about the specific steps for your area. And never flush old contact lenses down the toilet, as they will end up polluting waterways!

Use eco-friendly floss. Tiny pieces of floss can easily get scattered around the land and oceans. The solution: eco-friendly floss! There are many **eco-friendly flosses** on the market that are biodegradable.

Make your own juice. Instead of buying your juice of choice once a week at the grocery store, you can make your own **fresh juice** at home. You can either invest in a juicer or use a blender or food processor to make juice. Think of all the plastic containers you'll be keeping out of landfills by merely making your own juice in the mornings!

Start an **environmental group** in your area. While there are many organizations across the globe dedicated to environmental issues, starting your own local group is a great way to address issues that are important to you. Your group could tackle a myriad of issues, such as clean water, river or beach cleanups, or even spreading the word in your area about environmental issues.

Buy a hybrid car. A hybrid car, which uses an electric motor to reduce the dependency on gasoline for power, produces fewer gas emissions and gets better gas mileage. Next time you're in the market for a new car, **think hybrid**!

Don't buy feather accessories. **Feathers** for products like feather dusters, hair extensions, and boas are often removed from birds unnaturally. Feathers look best on their rightful owners, so please opt for cruelty-free synthetic feather items!

Support **wetland conservation**. Wetland conservation is meant to protect areas where water exists at or near the earth's surface, such as swamps and marshes. Wetlands are an important food source for thousands of people; in fact, they help provide wild rice, which is a staple for over half of the world's population. Wetlands also provide ecosystem services, such as water filtration and helping to reduce the impact of floods. Participate in programs that help protect and restore wetlands!

Say no to **hydraulic fracturing**. Hydraulic fracturing, otherwise known as fracking, is the process of breaking up rock formations underground to extract fossil fuels, such as oil and methane gas. Fracking is expensive, pollutes the environment, and is not a good long-term solution when clean, renewable energy is possible. Support environmental organizations that are standing up to big business in the fight against fracking. To save the planet we must speak up when we see something wrong!

Say no to drain clog removers. All those chemicals in clog removers aren't good for our **waterways**. If you have a clogged drain, try using a wire hanger, a plunger, or even baking soda and vinegar to clear it. It's important to be mindful of what you put down a drain—it all goes somewhere!

Boycott companies whose practices harm the environment. If you read about a company that is destroying forests for palm oil or funneling spring water away from natural resources, don't give them your money! **Vote with your dollar** in support of Mother Earth!

Don't support marine parks. Marine parks may say that the cetaceans in their captivity are healthy and happy, but according to data collected over the years, as well as the numerous deaths, this is not true. In the wild, orcas can travel up to 100 miles in a day, dive up to 200 feet, and spend most of their time deep under the water's surface. But in marine parks, they cannot do this. Please refrain from supporting and visiting marine parks and urge your friends and family to do the same! **Living in harmony with animals** is the best way to save our planet.

Make your own **dog treats**. By making your own dog treats you'll be able to control what goes into the treats, and you won't have to buy packaged dog treats every month. Your dog will love the homemade treats, and you'll avoid unnecessary plastic waste!

Follow your favorite environmental organizations on social media. Keeping up with leading organizations on *Twitter* and *Facebook* provides an easy way to stay informed and can offer suggestions for other ways you can take action on specific causes. Be sure to ask your friends and family to give environmental groups a follow on **social media** too!

Grow hydroponically. Hydroponics is a method of growing plants without any soil or in an aquatic-based environment. If you are low on space in your yard or just want to grow even more plants than you already are, growing hydroponically could be the solution for you. Innovative ways to grow plants make Mother Earth happy!

Adopt a highway. By adopting a highway, you'll commit to clearing the roads of litter, a perfect way to give back to the earth! If your area doesn't have an "Adopt a Highway" program, see if there are any environmental groups in your area that pick up litter along roadways. Every little bit helps!

Use every part of your food. Try saving the apple core and skins to make jelly. Use bruised tomatoes in recipes that call for chopped tomatoes. If you're peeling potatoes, make a snack by turning the peels into chips. The more resourceful we get in using every part of our food, the more we'll help **reduce food waste**!

Sponsor a farm animal. **Farm animal sanctuaries** are dedicated to sheltering farm animals that were abused or neglected. By "adopting" a farm animal at your local animal sanctuary you'll be covering the costs of medical care, feed, and shelter for the animal. Sponsoring a farm animal would also make a great gift for an animal lover, and since many sanctuaries offer virtual sponsorships, you won't even have to print anything out. Sponsoring a farm animal is a wonderful way to give back to the amazing animals that share our planet!

Recharge your gadgets' batteries properly. By understanding how to **recharge the batteries** in each of your devices properly, you'll be able to extend the life of the batteries. This means less electronic waste ending up in landfills!

Certify your backyard as a **wildlife habitat**. There are certain requirements that your yard must meet to be certified as a wildlife habitat, including providing a food source, a water source, and a safe place for wildlife to raise young. By having your yard certified, it further shows your commitment to helping wildlife and the environment!

Use your license plate to help environmental groups. You can apply for a special **license plate**, such as a personalized plate or a plate that helps the charity of your choosing. The charities or nonprofit organizations you can select will depend on where you live, but usually a part of the registration fee goes toward that organization's mission. Not only will you be donating to a cause, but you'll also get a new license plate so that everyone can see that you are passionate about environmental causes!

Make sure your car's exhaust system is up to date. Next time you bring your car in for an oil change, ask the mechanics to ensure that your exhaust system is up to date and perhaps see if there is a more **environmentally friendly system** available. It's important to make sure your car isn't spewing out unhealthy gases into the air every time you drive!

Run for local government. Instead of waiting for other people to act, use your power to make a difference in your community. If you're unhappy with how things are in your area, try running for local government. If you're not able to **run for local government** but still want to be involved in your area's politics, particularly in regard to environmental issues, attending meetings and voicing your opinion is always a great option.

Set your refrigerator and freezer to the right temperature. By using an incorrect setting, you could be guzzling more energy than necessary. Typically, refrigerators should be set between 37°F and 40°F, and freezers should be set at 5°F. Simply by making sure they are set at the **proper temperature**, you could save energy and, in turn, help the earth!

Say no to glue traps. Glue traps will often trap animals they aren't meant for and can cause unbearable suffering. Always opt for humane options when dealing with unwanted guests in your home, such as by blocking their entry into the home and removing their food sources by keeping your counters and floors clean. It's important to **be kind to all inhabitants** of the earth!

Upcycle old wine bottle corks. If you're a wine fan you've probably realized that **wine bottle corks** can be used for any number of projects. You could use the corks to make a corkboard, a picture frame, or even a business card holder. Don't let all of those corks go into the trash when you could take advantage and use them!

Don't buy shark teeth. Even though overfishing and the fin trade are driving shark species to extinction, shark teeth and jaws can be found in tourist shops in many seaside areas throughout the world. Do your part to **keep sharks alive** and happy by always refusing shark teeth!

Recycle old license plates. License plates are made out of aluminum, which means they are **recyclable**. Contact your local recycling plant to discover the best way to dispose of old license plates. You could also upcycle the license plates and make a collage photo frame. Whatever the case may be, don't just let old license plates go into the trash, where they are bound to wind up in our oceans or landfills!

Apply to jobs online. If you're in the market for a new job, **go the digital route**. Many companies and organizations offer a way to apply for jobs online instead of printing out multiple copies of your resume. The more we reduce our dependency on paper, the better off the environment will be!

Support sea turtle restoration efforts. **Sea turtles** are vital to our oceans because they help balance the food chain and assist with nutrient cycling. Unfortunately, sea turtle populations have been in a strong decline over the past 200 years. Support nonprofits that are dedicated to restoring sea turtle populations, either with a monetary donation or by volunteering at your local center.

Get your office involved. Suggest a **"volunteer day"** with your coworkers and spend the day volunteering at a local wildlife sanctuary. You can also incorporate environmentally friendly practices into your workspace by suggesting that your office ban Styrofoam and reduce the use of plastic.

Rearrange your furniture. If you place a lamp, a TV, or any item that heats up when in use near air vents, it could cause the air-conditioning to run longer to compensate. Take a look at the rooms in your house and see if any furniture could be rearranged to prevent this from happening. Another simple way to **cut back on energy use**!

Opt for **antibiotic-free meat**. High rates of antibiotic use could be contributing to antibiotic-resistant "superbugs," which are bacteria that have evolved to resist antibiotics. Superbugs could adversely affect human health and disrupt ecosystems. Be a smart consumer and make sure you know exactly where your food comes from!

Don't close vent registers in rooms you are not using. Many believe that by closing heat registers in a room they are not using, they will cut back on energy use. Unfortunately, most air-conditioning systems won't recognize when a register is closed and will still use the same amount of energy to cool or heat a room. Instead of closing registers, look into other ways to save energy, such as using your ceiling fan or **opening up the windows** when it's a nice day outside.

Put up a sign in your yard with an **eco-friendly message**. Ask your favorite environmental nonprofit if they have yard signs you can use free of charge, or make a custom sign yourself (make sure to use an environmentally friendly printing office). A yard sign that says, "There Is No Planet B" or "Save the Bees" could really get people thinking as they drive by!

Support your local botanical garden. **Botanical gardens** are vital to our ecosystems since biodiversity is being lost at an alarming rate. Botanical gardens work toward researching and conserving plants and habitats. Support your local botanical garden and its efforts to restore our ecosystems!

Take an online class on the weather. Learning all about how the weather works—from major storms and hurricanes to clouds and light precipitation—will allow for a better understanding of just how amazing our planet is, as well as help budding scientists learn to **track weather patterns and climate change**!

Watch the **sunrise or sunset**. Grab a blanket and head out to enjoy nature at its finest by watching a sunrise or a sunset. There is no better way to see nature's beauty and feel motivated to protect the earth!

Download a **"green app"** on your smartphone. Sometimes it's hard to see how much energy we are wasting in our households, but there are many "green apps" that will show you your energy usage per day. There are also apps for smartphones that control devices in your home; for example, if you forget to turn off the lights in the living room, the app will take care of it for you. The less energy we use, the happier the earth will be.

Try going **zero waste**. It may seem daunting, but going zero waste is not entirely impossible. Try going zero waste for one week, and once you've accomplished that goal, go zero waste for a month, and then a year!

Help **save rhinos from extinction**. Similar to elephants that are poached for their tusks, rhinos are often poached for their horns. The Javan and Sumatran species of rhino in Asia are critically endangered, with a subspecies of the Javan rhino declared extinct in Vietnam in 2011. The demand doesn't seem to be slowing down, with poachers even breaking into zoos to kill rhinos and take their horns. Spread awareness about rhinos to everyone you know. It's up to us to speak up for those that also share the planet with us!

Place a **birdbath** in your yard. You can find a birdbath at your local thrift store or try making one yourself and leave it in your yard for the birds to enjoy. Make sure to fill it daily and year-round, not just during the hotter months. You'll be providing the birds with a necessary water source and creating a beautiful scene that you can enjoy daily!

Invest in ramps for your pool to **save frogs**. If you have a pool (or know someone who does) then you know firsthand how sad it is to find a dead frog while cleaning your pool. To help them escape, you can purchase ramps that go from your pool to the sidewalk; that way, frogs and other small creatures can easily escape. When saving our planet, it's important to help animals too!

Use **cruise control**. Give your leg a rest and use the cruise control option on your car. Driving at a steady speed will help your car consume less fuel and will help improve your mileage by up to 15 percent.

Protest offshore drilling. **Offshore drilling** is typically done to extract petroleum, which is in rock formations beneath the seabed. Burning fossil fuels like petroleum contributes to carbon pollution and therefore climate change. Carbon pollution will also settle into the oceans, making waters more acidic and causing damage to coral reefs as well as shellfish and other marine animals. Offshore drilling must be replaced with clean, renewable energy if we want to maintain healthy oceans.

Talk to local farmers. Engage with your local farmers and ask how they grow their crops. It's easy to walk into a grocery store and not have any connection to the food you're buying, but by talking to local farmers, you'll get involved in the process and know exactly where your food comes from!

Look into **rooftop gardening**. If you live in an apartment, container gardening, window gardening, and vertical gardening are all possibilities that can give you some space to grow your favorite plants. Many buildings all over the world also have gardens on their roofs, a great way to utilize otherwise empty space. See if your landlord will allow you to create a rooftop garden for your apartment building. The more green spaces there are, the happier the planet will be!

Suggest sand or mulch instead of rubber mats in playground areas. Once we humans are done with them, rubber mats take years to biodegrade. Suggest that your city switch to **sand or mulch** in playground areas instead. The fewer toxic materials we use, the better off the environment will be.

Opt for plastic-free gum. Surprisingly, almost all chewing gum is made out of plastic. Thankfully, there are some that are **plastic-free**. Be a green consumer and do your research before buying a pack of gum!

Speak up for the **vaquita porpoise**. Vaquitas are native to the Gulf of Mexico, and due to human interference, like fishing, there are fewer than thirty vaquitas left in the entire world. We are on the verge of losing them forever unless we speak up. Support groups that are working to protect the vaquita species so that they can continue to live in their natural environment. And be sure to spread the word to friends and family about these amazing animals before it's too late!

Protest seismic blasting. Seismic air guns are used to find oil and gas underneath the ocean floor. The noise negatively affects marine life by causing temporary or permanent hearing loss, which can cause marine animals to strand themselves on beaches, abandon their habitat, and experience disruption to their mating and feeding habits. Whales and dolphins rely on their hearing to find food, communicate, and reproduce, so if they can't hear, it is very much a life-or-death matter. If you hear about seismic blasting happening in your area, **speak up and voice your opinion**! In order to maintain a healthy planet, we must consider how our choices affect others.

Copy and print on both sides of paper. Most copiers and printers have settings that allow you to do this automatically. **Save paper**—and the trees it's made from—with this simple trick!

Support **Arctic sanctuaries**. The Artic is melting at an alarming rate due to global warming, and the area has very little protection against it. Support organizations that work to protect the Artic for future generations, including the Indigenous communities that rely on the Arctic.

Don't fertilize your yard. Nitrogen and phosphorous from fertilizers can enter lakes and aid in the growth of algae and aquatic plants. Eventually, this overgrowth will suffocate the lake and result in what are known as "dead zones," where aquatic life can't survive due to lack of oxygen. Instead of using fertilizers, opt for **eco-friendly landscaping practices**. This simple switch will make the earth smile!

Donate moving boxes. If you've just finished moving, see if a friend or family member needs any boxes. You could also try posting in local groups online to see if anyone needs boxes. This is a wonderful way not only to build community but also to **help the planet by reusing items**!

Support oyster restoration efforts. Due to poor water quality and habitat loss, oysters are yet another animal that needs our help to survive. There are efforts to place oysters in sanctuaries as well as manage oyster reserves. Healthy waters include **thriving ecosystems**, and by supporting oyster restoration efforts, you'll help create a happy environment!

Use luggage made out of recycled materials. Next time you're shopping around for luggage, consider eco-friendly luggage made out of recycled materials, like hemp or organic cotton. This will help **reduce your carbon footprint**!

Protect your gadgets. Make sure to invest in a sturdy case for your laptop, cell phone, and any other electronic devices. Broken devices often end up as **electronic waste**, which can have adverse effects on human health and the environment. Be kind to your gadgets!

If you have a septic tank, **check for leaks**. During routine maintenance for your septic tank, have the technician confirm that there are no leaks in the tank. A leaking septic tank is dangerous to both you and the environment!

Go rock climbing. You'll pick up a fun new skill while seeing the world from a whole new vantage point! **Take your camera** and snap some photos to share on social media. Your friends are sure to love the beautiful photos of nature!

Make your own lotion. The great thing about **homemade** lotions is that they are customizable to your needs and preferences. For example, try personalizing your recipe with your favorite essential oils. This way, you won't have any unfamiliar chemicals like you'll find in many of the lotions at the store—a win for both you and the earth!

Report illegal dumping. If you see someone dumping potentially hazardous chemicals in unauthorized areas, **immediately report it** to your local city waste office. Illegal dumping poses threats to human health and, of course, isn't very nice to our planet!

Don't run a half-empty load of **laundry**. Always do the washing when your laundry baskets are full to help conserve water.

Switch your current Internet home page to an energy-saving one. For instance, Google's "Blackle" will change the background of the search page to black to reduce the screen brightness, effectively **saving on energy use**!

Use **responsible mechanics**. When going to the auto repair shop for routine maintenance on your car, make sure the mechanics properly dispose of oil and other car chemicals. You don't want to inadvertently support such chemicals clogging up our waterways.

Travel by plane less. According to some estimates, one round-trip flight between New York and California can generate 20 percent of the greenhouse gases your car emits over the entire year. While traveling by plane is a necessity in some situations, try to use other forms of transportation, such as taking a boat or train to your destination. Being mindful of your **carbon footprint** while traveling is key when it comes to helping the earth!

Put a hair catcher in your shower drain. Your hair will get trapped in the catcher instead of clogging up the drain and pipes. Without a catcher, the hair could end up in waterways, harming **aquatic life** and polluting the water. Plus, if you use a hair catcher in the shower, you won't have to clean the drain as often, saving you from having to use nasty chemicals to de-clog the drain!

Cut holes in six-pack rings. Before recycling your plastic six-pack rings, make sure to cut up the holes so marine life doesn't get ensnared in them. Or better yet, wean yourself off products that come in plastic rings entirely and **save the oceans** from undesired plastic!

Boycott zoos. It's true that some zoos contribute in small ways to conserving species, but the majority of animal species in zoos are not on the endangered species list. Zoos exist mainly for profit, and babies are often bred when there isn't even enough room for them, resulting in "surplus" animals. Instead of supporting zoos, you can learn about animals by visiting an **animal sanctuary** or by watching nature documentaries. If we truly want to help the earth, keeping animals captive in cages for our entertainment must go!

Start a seed exchange. Save seeds from organic fruits and vegetables bought at the farmers' market and create your own **seed exchange** among fellow gardeners (a fun hobby to pick up). You'll save money since you won't have to buy seeds, and you'll help maintain organic foods that aren't made using GMOs.

Use a mop. While household inventions such as the wet mop are certainly easy to use, they also produce unnecessary waste. Instead of using disposable pads to clean the floor, use a standard mop. Think of all the disposable cleaning pads you'll keep out of the trash!

Create a **children's nature garden**. By creating a garden path in your backyard and labeling plants and trees, you can set up a tour for the kids in your neighborhood. This is a wonderful way to get the neighborhood engaged in environmental protection while teaching our next generation of leaders the importance of protecting the planet!

Take only photographs. Nature is certainly breathtaking, but always remember to take **only photographs** when enjoying time outside, rather than bringing rocks or seashells home with you. This will ensure that nature remains exactly how it is for years and generations to come.

🌿

Use a wood stove. EPA-certified **wood stoves** are energy efficient and clean burning. This simple act will save money and the planet at the same time!

Create an online fundraiser. Create an online fundraiser to raise money for an **environmental nonprofit**, perhaps to celebrate your birthday. You'll help spread awareness about important issues to your friends while raising vital money for a good cause!

Live centrally. You could potentially save a lot of gas simply by considering where you live in relation to where you work and shop!

Teach a class on your eco-friendly talent. Many community education centers around the world are looking for **volunteer teachers** to expand course offerings. Whether you're a plant-based chef, a social media wiz, or a master at zero-waste living, your skills can be utilized. Contact your local community education center to learn how you can teach a class of your own and use your talents to help the earth!

Vote. When the next election comes around in your area, research politicians who are passionate about protecting our planet and include environmentally friendly policies in their campaigns. **Vote** for representatives who have the environment's best interests at heart!

Add a pond to your garden. Ponds are a great way to attract wildlife to your yard. Some creatures, like bees, birds, and dragonflies, may come to the pond just for a quick sip of water. Others, such as frogs and newts, may call the pond home. Adding a pond to your yard will help with biodiversity, creating a neat little **ecosystem** right in your backyard!

Dry your foods. Many food items, such as fruits, vegetables, and herbs, can be dried, meaning the water is removed from the food as a way to preserve it. Drying your own food is a great way to take a stand against **industrial agriculture** by sourcing and preparing your own food right at home!

Celebrate at a wildlife sanctuary. Consider an **animal or wildlife sanctuary** as the venue for your next major celebration or event! Your guests will enjoy their time outdoors, and you'll be able to educate them about the animals, some of which they never may have seen in person.

Avoid using leaf blowers and other dust-producing equipment. Blowing dust into the air can diminish **air quality**, negatively affecting both humans and animals. If you're trying to rid your yard of leaves, use a rake instead to reduce your environmental impact.

Support nature preserves. Nature preserves are essential to protecting wildlife. During your visit you can try a new skill like birdwatching or simply **enjoy the beauty of nature**.

Make your own yogurt. Cut back on plastic use by purchasing the bigger tub of yogurt at the grocery store instead of multiple smaller containers. Or cut out the plastic altogether and **make your own yogurt** at home. It's easy to do, and you'll become more involved in the process of how your food is made.

Use email for special occasions. For birthdays and other celebrations, send an **e-card** instead of a paper card. The sentiment will still be felt, and you'll cut back on paper use!

Support parks in your area. Go ride a bike, read a book, walk your dog...whatever you choose, just get out there and **support green areas** in your town!

Use an **electric lawn mower**. Simply switching from a gas-powered mower to an electric one will reduce your dependency on gas and cut down on harmful emissions, and you'll be able to get the job done just as effectively.

Invest in a solar water heater. Water heating is the second-biggest energy expense in your home after heating and cooling. If you really want to up your green game and save money at the same time, a **solar water heater** is the way to go. You could build your own solar water heater or buy an energy-efficient solar model from your local home-improvement store. Whichever route you go, you'll surely cut down on energy use, effectively helping our planet along the way!

Use reusable earplugs. For airplane travel, concerts, or sleeping, opt for **reusable earplugs** instead of disposable ones. You could potentially save hundreds of tiny earplugs from ending up as trash!

Use biodegradable pots in your garden. While the disposable plastic containers plants sometimes come in can end up in landfills, biodegradable pots create no additional trash because you can simply plant the entire container. **Biodegradable pots** will not only break down in the soil, but they will also add nutrients to your plants as they do. This is an easy way to forgo plastic and cut back on waste.

Create a *Twitter* account and share eco-friendly facts and tips. Social media is one of the most effective ways to get your message seen by a large number of people. Set up a *Twitter* account (or choose another social media site) dedicated to environmental awareness and share statistics on animal extinction, global warming...you name it! *Twitter* and other social media sites also give insight into **"trending" topics**, which are subjects that are popular at any given time on the site. Check to see what's trending and share an environmental message about those high-interest subjects. You could potentially reach thousands of people with your message, all from the comfort of your home!

Recycle correctly. Rules may vary, but it's important to sort items into their proper bins. Do a bit of research on the rules in your area, and make sure all items are being recycled properly instead of thrown into the garbage.

Host a bake sale. By hosting a **bake sale** in your community, you can raise money for a cause that's important to you and educate passersby on a particular environmental topic!

Learn about off-the-grid living. Living off the grid (meaning no connections to sewer, water, or electrical lines) may not be practical for everyone, but you may be able to learn some new strategies to help our planet. Look for off-the-grid communities in your area to learn more about building a self-sustaining house of your own. **Living off the grid** is truly one of the most sustainable ways you can lessen your impact on the environment!

Have your home tested for lead. This is essential if you have an older home. If you do have **lead-based paint**, seek the help of professionals to remove and properly dispose of the lead so that you're not polluting the air.

Support bike-share programs. Cities worldwide have started to incorporate **bike-share programs**, where bicycles are available for rent at certain spots around town for the community's use. These programs are imperative to encourage citizens to ride bikes instead of relying on cars or other forms of transportation that hurt the environment!

Go canoeing or kayaking. Both sports have **minimal impact** on the water and its inhabitants and are great ways to appreciate nature!

Go to estate and garage sales. Estate sales occur when a family or an estate is liquidating their belongings, while garage sales occur when a person is selling items from their household to free up space. No need to buy new items and potentially create **plastic waste** when there are plenty of opportunities to purchase gently used items!

Opt for a metal spoon to stir your coffee. Rather than using plastic utensils or stirrers that will quickly make their way into the garbage, try using a **metal spoon** instead.

Get your news online. Almost all newspapers offer an online version nowadays, making it easier than ever to have news at your fingertips. Think of all the paper you'll save just by opting to **read news online**!

Call in to radio shows. If you are tuning in to a **radio show** and hear a comment about an important environmental issue, call in and voice your opinion. Tell the audience that you are a concerned citizen, and offer suggestions for ways they can help the planet.

Purchase jewelry carefully. "Blood diamonds" are diamonds mined in war zones, and purchasing them can hurt the local economy. When there is less demand, there will be less mining, which will help to keep our environment pristine! Instead of buying new jewelry often, purchase used or **antique jewelry**. And be sure to resell your old jewelry or donate the items to your local thrift store.

Create a rain garden. A rain garden collects water from hard surfaces, such as sidewalks, patios, and driveways, in a shallow depression or hole in your garden so that the water can filter back into the soil directly. Creating a **rain garden** will reduce storm water runoff, decrease flooding potential, and prevent pollutants from traveling into local streams and lakes. Creating a rain garden is a perfect way to help keep our planet beautiful!

Choose a plastic wrap alternative. Instead of purchasing plastic wrap, which will only end up in the garbage, opt for a **reusable food wrap** made from natural materials. You can even make your own! One way to do this is by using melted beeswax and cotton cloth. Imagine all of the plastic you'll keep out of landfills!

Make your own biosphere. The **biosphere** is the parts of the land, sea, and atmosphere where life exists. You can easily make a do-it-yourself, self-contained biosphere model in a mason jar, a fun project that will teach you all about the delicate balance of ecosystems!

Turn down or shut off your **water heater**. When you'll be away for extended periods of time, simply turn off your water heater. No need to waste energy if you won't even be home!

Make **cold food** when feasible. Opt for salads, sandwiches, and other cold meals over items that require the use of the microwave, stovetop, or oven. This way, you'll save on energy use since the food won't need to be heated up!

Donate money to an environmental charity. One of the best ways to help protect our planet is to support groups that are on the frontlines. Even **donating a dollar** every month would go a long way toward helping preserve forests, oceans, and other endangered areas! You'll feel good knowing your money is going to a worthwhile cause.

Ask for meetings with your **government representatives**. Writing to your local representatives is a great way to take action, but you could go a step further and ask to meet with them. Prepare information packets that include factsheets on proposed ordinances, and talk to your representatives about how you feel about environmental issues.

Add a sticker with an eco-friendly message to your laptop. You could also **add stickers** to your reusable water bottle, the back of your phone, or your mailbox. Spread the world about important environmental causes and show the world you care!

Be aware of greenwashing. **Greenwashing** is when a company or organization uses deceptive practices to convince the public that they are environmentally friendly. With the rise of consumer interest in green products and services, many companies want to appear eco-friendly and may exaggerate their level of eco-friendliness. Always doing your research into company and organizational practices is a simple way to do right by our planet!

Don't transport firewood long distances. Doing so could also transport invasive species to new locations. Instead, burn firewood where you buy it. Make sure to ask the firewood dealer were the wood was cut, and if it's more than 50 miles away, find another source of firewood. **Keep our forests happy** and intact for future generations to enjoy!

Use an eco-friendly garden hose. Some **garden hoses** are made with phthalates, lead, BPA, and other toxic materials that can be transferred to your garden or lawn through the water they spray. Opt for a garden hose that doesn't contain harmful chemicals or additives and you're already making a great step toward helping nature!

Reuse takeout containers. Next time you order takeout, wash the plastic containers and save them. You can use the containers to bring your lunch into work or store leftovers from dinner. Or get a little creative and try placing them under indoor plants to hold water. You could even save the containers and bring them back to the same restaurant next time you order food. You'll be saving the containers from ending up in the landfill, all while reusing them for another purpose. Every little bit counts!

Save the earthworms. You've probably seen **earthworms** come out onto the pavement after a heavy rain. When you see one on the sidewalk, gently move it to nearby grass. Earthworms are vital to the ecosystem because the tunnels they dig create pores for oxygen, allow water to enter, and offer ways for carbon dioxide to leave the soil. Next time you see an earthworm struggling on the pavement, help it out!

Keep the oven door **closed**. By opening the door, you are letting heat escape. When you close it again, the oven has to work to bring the temperature back up to where it was. If you have a window on your oven, check food by looking through the window so heat doesn't escape through an open door!

Use eco-friendly cosmetics. Revamp your makeup routine and choose cosmetics that are organic, meaning the ingredients come from farming without chemical fertilizers, pesticides, or added toxins or hormones. You might also want to look for cosmetic brands that use minimal packaging or that donate a portion of profits to environmental charities. The rise in **cruelty-free cosmetics** has also led to many beauty brands forgoing animal testing and not including animal ingredients in their products. It's possible to be earth-friendly in all aspects of our lives!

Use e-gift cards. Instead of buying a physical gift card, many stores now offer **electronic gift cards**. All the gift recipient has to do is show the e-gift card to the cashier on their phone. This act could potentially save thousands of gift cards from being thrown out!

Invest in **solar panels** for your home. Power your house using the unlimited, reliable resource of the sun and save on energy use. Depending on where you live, there may be incentives like tax breaks.

Wear T-shirts with eco-friendly messages. Help the planet whether you're shopping, at the ball game, or taking a hike by simply wearing an **eco-friendly message** on your clothes. Everyone who passes you will see the important message. It's vital that we always speak up for the earth!

Carry an extra **reusable shopping bag** to the store in case someone else doesn't have one. It's easy to forget your reusable bag, so keep an extra one handy in case a fellow shopper is in need. And if you're the one who is always forgetting the reusable bags, perhaps get a small reusable shopping bag that you can keep in your purse or another spot where you won't forget it!

Choose your **sunscreen** carefully. Some sunscreens contain chemical UV filters that aren't healthy for you or the environment. When the chemicals end up in waterways, it's possible for them to disrupt the hormonal balance of animals. These chemicals are also responsible for coral bleaching. Remember to look for chemical-free sunscreen in glass containers to prevent plastic waste. Next time you go out to enjoy the sunshine, be mindful of the sunscreen you use!

Go to a stylist who uses **natural products**. If you're going to the salon to have your hair cut or colored, ensure that your stylist is using hair products that are free from synthetic chemicals and ammonia. Using a green salon will also show your friends and family how easy it is to be green and help the environment even when you're getting a haircut!

Recycle bread tags. Keep a jar and save all of the plastic tags from the packaging on loaves of bread, and ask your family and friends to do the same. The funds you earn from bringing those tags to the recycling facility could be donated to a **community environmental project**. You could also repurpose bread tags as bookmarks, labels for the plants in your garden, or markers to differentiate your keys. Instead of having those tiny little tags end up in our landfills and oceans, they can be put to good use!

Support restaurants that serve **locally grown food**. There is quite a bit that happens before your food ends up on your plate, including heavy water and land use and lots of transportation between locations. By supporting locally grown food, you're helping local farmers and shortening the distance between the food and your table.

Use cold frames in your garden. A **cold frame** is a box with sides made of brick, straw bales, or wood and a clear top. The walls help protect your crops from the cold, while the clear top lets in sunlight. Using cold frames in your garden will help extend your growing season, reduce packaging waste, and cut down the amount of fuel for transportation!

Use **eco-friendly soap** if you're bathing in a lake. Taking a dip in a lake is refreshing, but washing your hair outdoors isn't environmentally friendly. Soaps and shampoos contain pollutants that are harmful to the organisms living in the water. Be mindful of our scaled friends!

Find free advertising space. Many newspapers, magazines, and billboard companies will donate unused space to nonprofit organizations. All you have to do is call around to various **advertising agencies** in your area and see what's available. Thousands of people could easily see a positive, eco-friendly message!

Humanely deal with yellow jackets. Getting stung by a yellow jacket is not fun by any means, but they aren't all bad. Yellow jackets are predatory insects, so they help **control garden pests**. Since yellow jackets tend to nest in the ground or in old piles of wood, you can easily prevent them from living in your yard by creating a well-mulched garden and removing any woodpiles. Always remember to live in harmony with animals; they all play a role in our ecosystem!

Protect bats from barbed wire. Not only are bats great at insect control, but they are also wonderful **pollinators**. Unfortunately, bats—and other animals—often get stuck on barbed wire. Say no to barbed wire and help educate others on why we need bats!

Protect rainforests. Rainforests are disappearing at a rapid rate, due in part to industrial animal agriculture, also known as factory farming. Support organizations that are on the ground working toward conserving rainforests!

Say no to GMOs. According to the World Health Organization, **genetically modified organisms** have been altered in a non-natural way. GMOs are used to make a plant insect resistant, herbicide resistant, or even virus resistant. The research surrounding GMOs is conflicting, but there is evidence that connects GMOs with environmental damage and health issues. GMOs may be toxic to bees and butterflies, which puts biodiversity at risk. Choose products that note they are GMO-free!

Love leftovers. Don't let any food go to waste! If you have **leftovers** from a meal, place them in a reusable container and you already have lunch ready for tomorrow.

Save the water from your **dehumidifier**. If you use a dehumidifier, save the water it gathers to water your plants. This effortless act could save gallons of water!

Buy the right amount of paint. By knowing exactly how much **paint** you need for a specific job, you won't be wasting paint and potentially dumping toxic chemicals.

Donate to a food bank. Many grocery stores will throw away dented canned food or bruised produce, but if you politely ask the store manager for the items, they will more than likely give them to you free of charge. Donate the items to your local **food bank** for people in need. Monetary donations to your local food bank are also very much appreciated. Considering how much food is wasted around the world, we can all do our part to combat the issue!

Use cedar chips or aromatic herbs instead of mothballs in your closet. Traditional mothballs contain fumes and chemicals. Always use **natural alternatives** when you can to keep our planet happy and healthy!

Find an **eco-friendly nail salon**. If you go to a nail salon, make sure there aren't toxins in the polish or other products that could make them harmful to the planet. Protect your own health and that of the environment!

🍃

Insulate your water heater. Insulating your water heater using pre-cut jackets or blankets can reduce heat losses by up to 45 percent. By helping your water heater keep the temperature up, you'll **reduce energy use** and save money.

🍃

Say no to pizza "package savers." Many pizza restaurants will place what is known as a "package saver" in the middle of the pizza so the top of the box won't touch the food. When you order to-go pizza, politely ask that they don't include one with your order. Reducing your use of **single-use plastic items** will help protect marine life!

Use **e-coupons**. Many stores offer their coupons online, so instead of printing them out, you can just download the coupons you need onto your smartphone for the cashier to scan directly. If you receive coupons in the mail, make sure to opt out of the mailings. Small acts such as this add up when reducing paper use!

Use organic mulch in your garden. **Organic mulch** can range from grass clippings or compost to straw or shredded leaves. When it decomposes, organic mulch will improve your soil fertility and its organic content.

Learn to sew. If you know how to sew, you can fix many clothing items before they reach their end. If your pants have a rip in them or a sweater is missing a button, fix it! Extend the life of clothes so they don't end up in landfills.

Use an eco-friendly doormat. Help keep rubber and plastic out of landfills by using a doormat that is made out of **natural fibers or recycled items,** such as old tires or flip flops, instead of a doormat made out of new rubber and vinyl.

Support sustainable fisheries. **Sustainable fisheries** rotate among multiple species of fish and work to safeguard the health of our oceans. The ocean plays a massive role in regulating temperatures, weather patterns, and climate, with about half of the planet's oxygen coming from the sea. We must protect the ocean and its inhabitants from overfishing! Ask your favorite grocery store or restaurant if they serve sustainable fish, and if not, suggest that they do!

Buy laundry detergent and dish soap in boxes instead of plastic bottles. **Cardboard boxes** can easily be recycled and made into many more products than plastic!

Monitor species in your area. Contact your local conservation center and ask about **species monitoring**. There are thousands of volunteers worldwide who observe and record animals, such as monarchs, turtles, bears, and deer. This will help conservation centers know if their efforts are helping, which is crucial if we want to protect animals.

Sponsor a speaker. Many local schools and civic clubs will gladly host a speaker. See if there are any prominent **environmental leaders** in your area who would be willing to give a talk. At the talk, you could also set up a table to provide more information as well as ask for donations to go to a relevant nonprofit. This is an effective way to educate many on the environmental issues our planet is facing.

Always properly **recycle glass**. Unrecycled glass that ends up in landfills can take millions of years to decompose.

Donate **rubber bands**. If you have a bunch of rubber bands lying around and don't know what to do with them, donate them to a teacher who can use them for student projects. The post office will also gladly take rubber bands. You'll save hundreds of rubber bands from ending up in landfills!

Use cloth napkins. Instead of buying paper napkins, use **cloth napkins** and simply put them in the wash when they become dirty. Think of all the napkins you'll save from being thrown out!

Use paper tape. When mailing large items, use **paper tape** instead of plastic. This simple switch will help reduce your dependency on plastic!

Share an environmental message on your website. If you have a blog or website, place banners for your visitors to see. Many nonprofits have web banners already designed; all you have to do is ask if you can use them! You can also change your *Facebook* or *Twitter* cover photos to share an eco-friendly message. **Spreading awareness** is key!

Use eco-friendly trash bags. Using recycled plastic trash bags would certainly limit your plastic use, but you could even go a step further and use a **compostable trash bag** made from bio-based plastics. Compostable bags (such as the BioBag) are made from a combination of plant starches and fossil-based plastics and are certified to biodegrade in an industrial compost facility. Whichever you choose, you'll be reducing your plastic use, and that's a definite plus for the environment!

Suggest that your church become **fair trade certified**. There are many churches worldwide that are registered as "fair trade churches," meaning they use fair trade products, such as sustainably sourced tea and coffee. Fair trade churches also promote fair trade events and worship to promote eco-friendly practices. If your church isn't already registered as fair trade, make a suggestion! You could help make a difference in the lives of many people as well as the environment.

Install **low-flow faucets** in your home. Switching the faucets in your home to a low-flow option is an easy way to lower your water consumption while saving money!

Properly recycle tires. When your car's **tires** need to be replaced, don't send them to a landfill where they will sit around for years (or worse, be dumped into lakes or abandoned lots). Instead, contact your local recycling facility or tire recycle shop.

Hold a demonstration. One effective way to speak up for the environment is by holding a **peaceful demonstration**. All you need are some posters with catchy slogans and some friends, and you could reach hundreds in your area. Holding a peaceful demonstration is also beneficial because you can send out a press release to encourage local media to cover your event, getting the message out to even more people!

Create your own local public-access television show. **Public-access television** is a form of media where the general public can create their own programming. Get some friends together and produce your own TV show to highlight environmental issues! You could even feature local experts, such as wildlife rehabilitators. Educate hundreds of people in your area on environmental issues that matter!

Offer to help out on a **class field trip** to a recycling facility. Seeing firsthand how products are recycled is a great opportunity for children. Or agree to support your child's teacher with an in-class activity that will teach about plastic pollution or the importance of helping wildlife. Getting kids involved in helping the environment is vital if we want to create a better future!

Use your wedding registry to ask for contributions to a nonprofit organization. If you're getting married, you can support your favorite environmentally friendly organizations by asking for **donations** instead of wedding gifts. Nonprofits are only able to continue doing lifesaving work, like protecting our coastlines and defending our air, because of donations. You'll also reduce paper use because you won't require gift receipts!

Choose glass containers for condiments. For ketchup, mustard, salad dressings, and other condiments, **choose glass over plastic**. If you really want to reduce your consumption, you can easily make your own condiments at home!

Take the train. Public transportation is always a great alternative when trying to **reduce your carbon footprint**!

Pickle your vegetables. The process of **pickling vegetables** has been around for thousands of years and is used by many cultures. Learn how to preserve your crops by pickling them and you won't have to buy prepackaged vegetables at the store!

Always report illegal hunting and fishing. If you witness illegal hunting or fishing, immediately report the incident to your local law enforcement. Illegal hunting and fishing can cause unbalanced **ecosystems**, so it's vital that we speak up if we suspect something is wrong.

🍃

Intern. One way to show you're a dedicated environmentalist is by interning at a nonprofit organization that works to protect the earth. You'll not only gain experience, but you'll also be directly helping their **lifesaving missions** to save our planet!

🍃

Make your own gifts. Get crafty! Not only is it thoughtful to make a **homemade gift** for someone, but you can also repurpose bags, fabric, and other items. Reusing items is key when helping the environment!

Keep heat and air-conditioning at a consistent temperature. You may think you're saving energy by turning off your heat or air-conditioning once you reach a comfortable temperature, but by continually turning it on and off, you're actually using more energy when it has to fully restart. Keep the temperature consistent and use other tricks to moderate the temperature, such as using a ceiling fan, opening up the windows when it's a nice day out, and utilizing the **energy-saving functions** on some air-conditioners. Little acts such as this will really add up to save energy!

Wash your clothes with warm or cold water instead of hot water. Your clothes will get just as clean and you'll be **saving energy**!

Perform **regular maintenance** on all appliances. If all the parts are in top working order, your appliances will last longer and you'll save energy!

Save **Styrofoam**. It's best to avoid use of Styrofoam altogether, but if you find yourself with some, cut it up into tiny pieces and reuse it as packing material. You could also use Styrofoam for plant drainage simply by cutting it into pieces and placing it at the bottom of pots and planters. It's an easy way to reuse materials and keep Mother Nature clean and healthy!

Learn to sail. Sailing is an excellent way to spend the afternoon enjoying the ocean. What's more, you won't be harming the environment with an electric motor since a sailboat is **wind-powered**. So get out there and see all of what nature has to give!

Grow more indoor plants in your home. If you don't have the space for a garden (or if you just like having plants around), indoor plants are a great option. **Indoor plants** both purify the air and act as a natural air-conditioning system, which would save on energy use compared to mechanized appliances.

Use bamboo toilet paper. Bamboo is a rapidly renewable source, and by using **bamboo toilet paper**, you'll be reducing your dependency on trees.

Clean light bulbs regularly. By cleaning your **light bulbs**, you'll help the bulbs last longer. You won't have to buy light bulbs as often, and you'll reduce unnecessary waste!

Introduce a **plastic bag ban** or tax. Several countries all over the world already have some form of ban or tax on plastic bags. If your area doesn't have one already, urge your elected officials to support legislation to make plastic bags undesirable. Your city could cut back on millions of plastic bags just by enacting a ban or a tax!

Leave shells at the beach. Shells are certainly beautiful, but don't pick them up and take them with you. By taking the shells, you're potentially harming the **aquatic ecosystem** since hermit crabs use them as homes, small fish will hide in them, and birds use shells to build their nests. Leave the shells where you found them to help out our aquatic friends!

Support **meat-free lunches** at local public schools. Meat-free lunch initiatives have been cropping up at public schools worldwide over the past few years, and the trend doesn't seem to be slowing down. Reducing meat consumption is critical if we don't want our children growing up in a world with pollution and food shortages. Contact Meat Free Monday or the Meatless Monday campaigns, both of which offer a plethora of resources for suggesting meat-free meals at your child's school, including tips for students and ideas for teachers!

Ditch aerosol sprays. **Aerosol** contributes to the depletion of the ozone layer and can be found in everyday items that are sprayed, such as deodorant, sunscreen, and air fresheners. Switch to non-spray options, such as creams and pump-spritz products. And if you have an empty aerosol can, make sure you properly recycle it at your local recycling center. This simple move away from aerosol sprays will help keep our planet's ozone layer happy and healthy!

Use wire hangers. Instead of buying plastic hangers, opt for **wire hangers**. This simple change will greatly reduce your plastic consumption.

Participate in Earth Day. Every year, April 22 is celebrated as **Earth Day**, a day designated to raise awareness about environmental protection. Some communities even celebrate Earth Week! Research any local events or demonstrations happening in your area in support of Earth Day and show your love for Mother Nature!

Make sure your car tires are **properly inflated**. This will ensure the longevity of your car as well as help you get better gas mileage!

When shopping, look for products with minimal to zero packaging, like fresh fruits and vegetables. Since many types of junk food come in **heavy packaging**, you'll more than likely eat healthier too!

⬥

Choose milk and orange juice in **glass containers**. The containers will probably have unrecyclable plastic caps, but opting for glass is a much more sustainable choice compared to plastic.

⬥

Wait to **preheat** your oven. Don't preheat the oven while you get the ingredients together. Save energy by preheating only once you're ready to cook!

Shred netting before disposing of it. If you're about to throw out an apple bag, potato bag, or any other type of netting, make sure to shred the netting before you do so. **Marine life** can wind up entangled in the netting and face a high risk of death.

Know what's in your refrigerator. It's easy to forget food you've purchased until it's all the way in the back of the refrigerator and already spoiled. **Reduce food waste** by planning out your meals each week so no items go uneaten.

Give this book to someone else! Or donate a copy to your local library, civic center, or college. Everyone can make a difference in protecting **Mother Earth**!